WICCA

NATURAL MAGIC KIT

THE SUN, THE MOON, AND THE ELEMENTS

Elemental Magic, Moon Magic, and Wheel of the Year Magic

LISA CHAMBERLAIN

Wicca Natural Magic Kit:
The Sun, The Moon, and the Elements

Published by **Chamberlain Publications (Wicca Shorts)**

ISBN-13: 978-1-912715-48-0

Disclaimer

YOUR FREE GIFT

Thank you for adding this book to your Wiccan library! To learn more, why not join Lisa's Wiccan community and get an exclusive, free spell book?

The book is a great starting point for anyone looking to try their hand at practicing magic. The ten beginner-friendly spells can help you to create a positive atmosphere within your home, protect yourself from negativity, and attract love, health, and prosperity.

Little Book of Spells is now available to read on your laptop, phone, tablet, Kindle or Nook device!

To download, simply visit the following link:

www.wiccaliving.com/bonus

GET THREE
FREE AUDIOBOOKS
FROM LISA CHAMBERLAIN

Did you know that all of Lisa's books are available in audiobook format? Best of all, you can get **three audiobooks completely free** as part of a 30-day trial with Audible.

Wicca Starter Kit contains three of Lisa's most popular books for beginning Wiccans, all in one convenient place. It's the best and easiest way to learn more about Wicca while also taking audiobooks for a spin! Simply visit:

<u>www.wiccaliving.com/free-wiccan-audiobooks</u>

Alternatively, *Spellbook Starter Kit* is the ideal option for building your magical repertoire using candle and color magic, crystals and mineral stones, and magical herbs. Three spellbooks —over 150 spells—are available in one free volume, here:

<u>www.wiccaliving.com/free-spell-audiobooks</u>

Audible members receive free audiobooks every month, as well as exclusive discounts. It's a great way to experiment and see if audiobook learning works for you.

If you're not satisfied, you can cancel anytime within the trial period. You won't be charged, and you can still keep your books!

INTRODUCTION

Congratulations on your decision to invest in *The Natural Magic Kit*. Together, these three books will help you expand your practice of magic within the framework of Wicca, Witchcraft, and other Pagan traditions.

The "Old Religion" is all about revering Nature and tapping its infinite energies, and these books invite you to dive into a deeper understanding of three core areas of spiritual and magical practice: the Elements, the Moon, and the Earth's revolving journey around the Sun.

This collection is intended for beginners and more seasoned Witches alike, and is accessible to anyone interested in integrating the power of Nature into their magical practice. Each contains spells, rituals, and other magical workings that will help you open up amazing pathways to a deeper connection with the Universe, and enhance your quality of life.

Elemental Magic offers a view of Wiccan-oriented ritual and magic through the lens of the Elements: Earth, Air, Fire, Water, and Spirit. By attuning to and working with the magical qualities of the Elements, we can manifest positive change and foster a deeper spiritual connection to the natural world. Of course, the Elements are part of many Pagan spiritual systems, and non-Wiccan readers will still find plenty of interesting discussion here.

The book will introduce you to each of the Elements: their properties, characteristics, magical associations, and effects on our lives. You'll learn how the Elements are invoked in ritual, as well as some techniques and magical practices for working with each Element individually. Of course, you'll also find spells, rituals and charms focused on each Element. Ultimately, *Elemental Magic* is a reference, magical guide, and inspirational springboard for you to make your own discoveries about the power of the Elements and the magic they have to offer.

Moon Magic is for anyone wanting to learn more about the connections between the Moon and the practice of magic, regardless of religious or spiritual orientation. While specific elements of Wiccan practice, like the Moon and the Triple Goddess, the celebration of Esbats, and the sacred act of drawing down the Moon are touched on here, the larger focus is on the power of the Moon itself and the benefits of an approach to magic that is aligned with the lunar cycle.

From New to Full, to Dark and back to New again, the never-ending cycle of the Moon presents wonderful opportunities to tune in to the energies of the natural world and enhance your spellwork. To that end, you'll find a detailed breakdown of each phase of the lunar cycle, spells for each phase, and magical recipes, techniques, and correspondences—all focused on making the most out of your connection to the Moon's amazing power.

Wheel of the Year Magic is rooted in Wiccan practices, but much of it is applicable to Pagans of all stripes, as well as anyone who is simply curious about the rich traditions surrounding these milestones of the Old Religion. This book provides a brief overview of the Wheel of the Year and its development within Gardnerian Wicca, and offers a framework for approaching the practice of magic as part of your Sabbat celebrations.

You'll find detailed explorations of each Sabbat, including their significance within the context of the ever-changing seasons, the part they play in the mythological cycle of the Goddess and the God, and the spiritual themes they ask us to reflect upon as we celebrate them. You'll learn about the historical origins of each holiday and the associated traditions and practices that have been handed down over the centuries from our European pagan ancestors. And of course, you'll also find tips and ideas for holding your own Sabbat celebrations, and a few suggested spells and other magical workings that correspond with the themes and season of each holiday.

These books can be read in any order, so start wherever your intuition guides you. As you read through the collection, you will find that you can incorporate ideas from all three books into your practice—observing the cycles of the Sun, Earth, and Moon, and tuning in to the ever-present energies of the Elements. So whether you follow a particular tradition of Wicca, Witchcraft, or another Pagan path, or an eclectic combination of all three—or even if you're simply just curious!—may you find wisdom and magical inspiration within these pages.

Blessed Be.

OVERVIEW

The *Natural Magic Kit* consists of the following three books:

WICCA

ELEMENTAL MAGIC

A Guide to the Elements, Witchcraft, and Magic Spells

LISA CHAMBERLAIN

CONTENTS

INTRODUCTION

What do magical spells, wishing wells, rain dances, and lucky rabbit's feet have in common? All of these customs are rooted in the idea that unseen forces can have an influence on the occurrences of our daily lives.

Even in this modern age of science and "reason," people still give at least some credence to superstitions: we cross our fingers and knock on wood for luck, and we avoid walking under ladders to prevent bad luck.

Whether we are conscious of it or not, all of these ideas and traditions are tied to underlying properties of the energy that makes up the entire Universe. This energy is found in everything on Earth, visible and invisible, including every human being. This energy is particularly essential to Witchcraft, and is the main focus of this book.

As interest in Wicca and other forms of Witchcraft continues to grow, interested readers will find a vast array of information about the Craft and its rich, varied beliefs and traditions. From coven-oriented, highly structured forms of Wicca to looser, eclectic and solitary forms of practice, people from all across the spectrum are sharing their knowledge with those who feel pulled in the direction of what many call "The Old Religion."

Terminology across these sources will vary, with some authors distinguishing between "Wicca" and "Witchcraft," and some making no distinction at all. This is just the way it is with Wicca: with no sacred text to study, many Wiccans end up taking their own, often very unique, journey as they discover the religion for themselves. This means that two authors can write on the same topic from completely different perspectives—it all depends on the author's personal beliefs, knowledge, and experiences.

With this in mind, there is no right or wrong, and this partly explains why there are so many differing—and on occasion, conflicting—opinions to be heard. For example, some Wiccans will practice Witchcraft actively, as part of their daily lives; however, other Wiccans will *never* participate in Witchcraft, and disassociate from it completely. Both are perfectly valid approaches—my advice to you is to take in as much information as possible, and then form your own set of beliefs based on the ideas and practices that resonate most with you.

This particular book offers a view of Wiccan-oriented ritual and magic through the lens of the Elements—Earth, Air, Fire and Water, as well as Spirit, the Fifth Element—and is intended for beginners and more seasoned Witches alike.

For thousands of years, the Elements have been considered the basic building blocks of the Universe, and they are inherent to the basic principles of Witchcraft. Wiccans and other Witches recognize, honor and participate with these core energies in both religious ritual and magic. By attuning to and working with the magical qualities of the Elements, both individually and combined, Witches are able to manifest positive changes for themselves and others, fostering a deeper spiritual connection to the natural world.

One way of tuning in to that connection is through an understanding of the principle of *animism*, which is a major concept this guide to Elemental magic will discuss.

A concept that has spanned the cultures of the globe for millennia, animism takes for granted that there is more to the material world than we can grasp with our usual five senses. Some Witches have also always taken this for granted, but many have to study and practice for awhile before finding themselves grounded in what is for them, coming from contemporary culture, a new reality.

This is where getting to know the Elements on a more intimate level can be very helpful.

This book will introduce you to each of the Elements: their properties, characteristics, and their use in magic. You'll learn how the

Elements are invoked in ritual, as well as some techniques and magical practices for working with individual Elements.

This book is by no means an exhaustive source of information, and the ideas it presents should never be considered the "way things are always done," but should instead provide you with a springboard to make your own discoveries about the power of the Elements and the magic they have to offer.

Blessed Be.

PART ONE
INTRODUCTION TO THE ELEMENTS

ELEMENTS AND THE LIVING UNIVERSE

What do the Elements have to do with our modern way of life?

Particularly in the developed countries of the West, it may seem that the answer is "*not much.*" Apart from weather events that can cause major inconveniences and the occasional catastrophe, we live life relatively removed from the basic forces of nature.

Even if we rarely think about it on a conscious level, we all understand how important the four Elements—Earth, Air, Fire, and Water—are for our survival. We need air to breathe, of course, and water to sustain life. We live on the Earth and depend on it as a source of food for sustenance, and fire—in the form of light, heat, and energy—is quite essential.

However, despite acknowledging their fundamental importance, most of us remain incredibly detached from the Elements.

We no longer have to build fires to heat our homes during the cold Winter months, and we can even keep out the sweltering Summer air with insulation. We have no need to worry about sourcing water, which is as easy as turning on a tap. Furthermore, most of us are very far removed from the sources of our food, and there's an enormous variety of "food" products on grocery store shelves with ingredients that do even not come naturally from the Earth.

It almost seems as if we've gone to great lengths in the "civilized world" to get as far away from the Elements as possible. After all, they can be detrimental to our health and safety in many ways, as we can see in the phrase "exposure to the elements," which is often used in the context of damage or death.

What Witches know is that the Elements are powerful forces in their own right, with benevolent as well as destructive properties. They are necessary for the functioning of all life, even though they can be dangerous.

The Elements are perhaps the ultimate expression of the co-creative nature of the Universe, as each interacts with all others in the physical realm, and each participates in its own way in the ongoing cycles of life and death. These forces are a fundamental part of Wicca and other nature-based religions, and they can, with practice and intention, be directed to cause a desired change in our lives—in fact, this is the essence of what magic and spellwork is.

But how do the Elements *work* in Witchcraft?

There are a number of ways to answer this, and different answers will come from different books, traditions, and individual practitioners. But a brief look at the lineage of Wiccan beliefs can help illuminate the general concepts that underlie the magic of the Elements.

ANCIENT CULTURES
AND THE NATURAL WORLD

While Wicca as a religion has quite modern origins, its beliefs and practices borrow from many older sources, including deities from ancient Egypt, India, Greece and Rome; holidays from old European pagan traditions; and magical lore from the Celtic world.

A key element of many of these older traditions is what anthropologists call *animism*. This term refers to a worldview that is very different from the mainstream worldview of most modern Western cultures.

Over the past few centuries, conventional science has shaped the modern perspective that the material world is *only* material, with no connection to the spiritual world (if, in fact, the spiritual world is even recognized at all). For those who don't believe in a spiritual world, the separation is seen as between mind and matter, an idea made popular by the philosopher Descartes in the 17th century.

The animistic perspective, by contrast, is that there is *no separation at all* between the material and spiritual worlds, and this belief underlies much of the work of Witchcraft.

The word "animism" is derived from the Latin *animus*, which means "soul" or "mind." In this orientation to the world, the quality of soul, or spirit, is not limited to humans or even all living creatures, but is found in all things.

Many animistic cultures view certain objects in the natural world—such as trees and other plants, springs and other bodies of water, and various geological formations—as having individual souls, or holding particularly strong spirit energy. These objects may be considered sacred to particular deities, or physical manifestations of unnamed spirits.

For example, in Greek mythology, humans were often transformed into trees and other plant life, where their spirits remained. Greek and Latin mythologies abound with various types of nymphs—female spirits who inhabit particular land forms, including trees and mountains, as well as bodies of water, the sky, and the Underworld. The Mayans are known to have prayed to the spirits of weather phenomena, such as clouds and lightning. And ancient goddesses and gods of Egypt were invoked into amulets and talismans worn for help with fertility, hunting, and other aspects of successful living.

In other words, the majority of ancient religions embraced animism, at least to some extent. As a result, animism is often said to be the fundamental basis from which later religions grew.

Now, for our hunter-gatherer ancestors, the relationship with nature was much more direct and intimate than it is for us today. While many of us may seek experience with the natural world through camping trips or long hikes, our ancestors lived their entire lives in "the great outdoors," where there really was no "material world" to stand in the way of communing with the spiritual—there was none of the noise of our modern world to drown out nature's messages. Instead, being in tune with the life force in all things was simply part of the human experience.

It is said that as hunter-gatherer societies gradually gave over to agriculturally based societies, animism became more elaborate, giving rise to deities who became responsible for particular aspects of the physical world. There are gods who rule over types of weather, as well as gods associated with human activity such as war, hunting, and the harvest. Some deities were assigned to the spiritual world, as well—such as **Hades**, who rules the Greek Underworld, and Arawn, the king of the Welsh Otherworld.

Although the rise of Christianity and Islam all but stamped out ancient religions in many parts of the world, animism has survived into modern times in various places.

In parts of Indonesia, where traditional indigenous cultural practices have been officially "outlawed," people still believe in the spirits of natural phenomena like trees and rocks, as well as rice, which is considered to have a soul similar to that of humans, and is grown and tended to with ceremonial rituals to ensure abundance.

In many Native American traditions, animals are an integral part of spiritual growth for those who walk the animist path. Alternately called animal totems or power animals, they serve as teachers, guides, and messengers for people on their journey through life.

Native American medicine also incorporates animism, as the sacred herbs involved in traditional healing are considered to have spirits themselves. These plants are treated with the utmost respect and are prayed to and thanked before they are picked for use in ritual. Some healers even have the ability to "hear" the plant spirits and thus learn their potential uses directly from the plant. This is how many indigenous peoples learned to use herbal medicine in the first place.

In Ireland, people still tie ribbons or strips of cloth to hawthorn trees, known as "wishing trees," as a form of prayer. Ancient springs and wells, whose waters are believed to contain the powers of the Otherworld, are found all across the Celtic Isles. These places were later renamed "holy wells" as Christianity merged with the indigenous Celtic religion.

The Irish landscape is also dotted with several enchanted places, which are often hills or ancient religious sites, where an invisible population of spirits, or "sidhe" (pronounced "shee") are said to live. The sidhe were the people who inhabited Ireland before the coming of the Celts, who "walked into the Earth" rather than surrender to their conquerors. Their dwellings are often called fairy forts or fairy mounds, and there are even places known as "fairy paths," where it's considered unwise to build homes or undertake any other construction.

Animism is a very general term—not a religion in and of itself, but a way of classifying religions and belief systems that are not monotheistic like most of today's major world religions. Each animistic tradition is unique to its own culture, and people in these cultures would not call themselves "animistic," since this is a Western term used to describe them from the outside.

From the inside, there is no need to have a term. It is taken for granted that the world is alive and full of spirits who are as connected with human life as the air itself, and that the energies of these spirits can be called on to help with the practical realities of daily life.

Witchcraft makes particular use of this last idea: that we can consciously communicate with the spiritual world and manifest positive changes in our circumstances, both on a personal level and for others.

Witches may do this largely through working with their own chosen deities, whether these deities have specific identities (such as Flora, the Roman goddess of flowers, or Cernunnos, the Irish god of wild animals) or are simply recognized as the Goddess and the God: the female and male creative energies that power the life cycles we witness on Earth year after year.

Some Witches may not actually believe in any deities *per se*, but instead commune with the spirits of the natural world as they understand them on an individual level. Some may even focus their spiritual and magical work simply through communing with the one force believed to be inherent throughout the Universe. They may call this force "the Universe," "the Spirit," "All That Is," or any other term that best describes their experience of these energies.

Most Wiccans and Witches, however, devote some degree of specific attention to the Elements in their practice, with a definite awareness of the spiritual presence inherent in each of these forces of nature.

MODERN OBSERVATIONS
OF THE NATURAL WORLD

Interestingly, some discoveries in the scientific fields seem to support aspects of the animistic perspective.

For example, it was demonstrated in the late 19th century by physicists Pierre and Jaques Currie that certain crystals, such as quartz and tourmaline, are piezoelectric. This means they can generate an electric charge when mechanical stress is applied, such as tapping them with a hammer. Some crystals also exhibit a pyroelectric effect, releasing an electric charge when exposed to a temperature change.

While these phenomena can be illustrated and described in purely "mechanical" terms, they also seem to point to a larger reality of crystals—that they are "alive" and participating in the ongoing creative force of the Universe in ways we can't see with the naked eye.

The practice of using crystals for emotional and physical healing, which dates back to ancient times and has seen a resurgence in recent decades, is rooted in this idea, and while their effectiveness has yet to be demonstrated by traditional scientific methods, there is plenty of testimony among users of these alternative healing modalities.

Another seeming convergence between scientific thought and the animistic paradigm is found in our evolving understanding of plant biology.

In the 1970s, a book called *The Secret Life of Plants*, by Peter Tompkins and Christopher Bird, described various experiments involving plants connected to polygraph machines. The machines registered the plants' apparent responses to the thoughts of people nearby, as well as to destructive behavior, such as stomping on another plant, an event that was apparently remembered by the plant "witness" after the fact. The book was widely discredited as "pseudo-science," but it helped promote the idea that plants are somehow influenced by external stimuli that would seem to have no logical effect on their behavior.

In the 21st century, some researchers are arguing that plants actually exhibit intelligence in various ways. For example, in one recent experiment, a plant exposed to a recording of a caterpillar chewing on a leaf produced chemicals used to defend against attack. In another, plants roots were observed to grow toward a buried pipe that was dry on the outside, but contained flowing water. Plants have at least three times the number of distinct senses as human beings, which enable them to sense and respond to everything in their environments, including chemicals in the air, different wavelengths of light, and other plant life in their vicinity.

One of the more fascinating discoveries has been the networks of "information exchange" observed in forests.

Scientists have been able to track the flow of nutrients and chemical signals exchanged along pathways through a "web" of fungi living underground. These studies have shown that older trees will share nutrients with younger trees that are still too shaded to get enough sunlight on their own, and that trees of one species will actually "cooperate" with other species by trading nutrients back and forth at different points in the growing season.

There has been intense debate among researchers in the plant sciences regarding the word "intelligence" as applied to plant life. Many scientists associate this word strictly with animals, and prefer terms like "electrical signaling" to anything that might suggest neurological activity, even though neurotransmitter chemicals such as dopamine and serotonin have been found in plants. But this is really an argument over the traditional scientific classifications of living organisms. The observed behavior of the plants themselves is not in dispute, and it offers an unprecedented glimpse into the invisible realms of the "inanimate" world.

Finally, there has been much interest in recent years in the work and publications of Dr. Masaro Emoto, a Japanese social scientist who turned his attention in the 1990s to the study of water.

Starting with the knowledge that no two snowflakes are identical, Emoto sought to find a way to view the molecular structure of water by freezing small samples of water from various sources, and then viewing it under a microscope as it began to thaw. After some trial and error, he was successful—hexagonal crystals emerged under the microscope, expanding three dimensionally as the water began to thaw, and then disappearing as the water returned to liquid form.

Emoto then began to experiment by using different stimuli on the water before freezing it, to see whether the appearance of the crystals would be affected. In particular, he tried exposing the water samples to visual images, verbal and written messages in various languages, as well as music and prayer.

The results he shared were astounding to many: water which had been subjected to positive messages and prayer formed more complete, aesthetically pleasing crystals, while water which had been exposed to negative messaging and negative emotions produced less complete and misshapen crystals.

Emoto documented these experiments with photographs that were published in a series of books called *Messages From Water*, along with his interpretations of the results: that water responds to the energetic charge of words, thoughts, emotions, and even art forms. Since water makes up around 70% of the human body, the implications for our own well-being when it comes to thoughts and feelings are important.

Another significant finding was that the source of the water being examined made a difference—water from more pristine sources, such as a waterfall in rural Japan, produced higher-quality crystals and with more consistency than tap water from urban sources, which tended not to produce any at all.

Emoto described the phenomena he observed in the context of his theory of "Hado," a term based on the Japanese ideograms for both "move" and "wave." Hado is essentially the subatomic vibrational quality of all matter in the Universe. It can be thought of as similar to "chi," but Hado as a concept is more centered on the relationship between human consciousness and the rest of existence.

The theory of Hado recognizes that thoughts and feelings are physical matter, and that changing our own vibrational energy can change the material world. Using this concept, Emoto and a few hundred of his supporters performed a prayer healing of a large, polluted lake in West Japan that resulted in significant reduction of the algae and odor that have plagued the lake every summer for decades. Emoto has used his discoveries to promote the importance of taking care of our water as a global resource.

Of course, conventional science has dismissed Emoto's work due to its lack of sufficient adherence to the scientific method. Emoto doesn't claim that his work meets these standards, but the results have been astounding enough to defy any "rational" explanation that the scientific model can currently offer. But in the realm of quantum physics, the theory of Hado doesn't appear to be so far-fetched.

It has parallels with ideas in newer, more cutting-edge scientific theories that also recognize the vibrational nature of matter and describe the most fundamental "building block" of matter as being, essentially, information, or "mental energy."

One physicist, Nick Herbert, has argued that mind permeates all of reality, and actually uses the term "quantum animism" to describe this fundamental quality of the Universe. Indeed, it seems that Descartes' conviction that mind is separate from matter, which has been so entrenched in Western scientific thought, is now being turned on its head.

ANIMISM, THE ELEMENTS, AND WITCHCRAFT

Of course, Witches don't need scientific proof of the animistic nature of the Universe in order to know that it is at work in all aspects of life.

They learn from their own experiments how to communicate with crystals, plants and water, as well as air and fire. The Craft is about revering nature in all its forms, and harnessing the vibrational power of *All That Is* to create positive change.

Working with a particular crystal, for example, Witches might hold the stone in both hands for a few moments and attune with its energies. Many people—not just Witches, Wiccans, and Pagans—have experienced differing sensations from holding different types of crystals in healing and spiritual work. Some crystals, like pyrite, can feel very energetic and "buzzy," while others, like moss agate, have a calming effect.

In addition to physical, spiritual and emotional healing, these Earth energies provide pathways to magical change. Pyrite, for example, is often used in magical work for self-confidence and wealth. Moss agate protects the aura from negative energy.

Water is traditionally part of every Wiccan ritual, either physically present or symbolically represented by a cup, a chalice, or a cauldron.

The water can even be a focus of the ritual, charged with the Witch's personal power for a particular intention. Some spells involve magical drinking water, charged with the energies of crystals or herbs. Water is also a scrying tool—Witches can gaze at the surface of a cauldron of water for images that communicate information from the unseen realms.

Air, being invisible, seems to be a much less tangible Element, but it often makes its presence known nonetheless. Sometimes it's subtle, and sometimes it's impossible to ignore.

Poets and Witches alike have invoked the wind and recognized its "personalities," from gentle to fierce, and it's not an uncommon thing to feel a particular "energy" in the air, especially just before a good storm. Wind works very symbiotically with the four directions, and the particular direction the wind is coming from at a given time can be more useful for particular magical work. For example, Western winds are good for strengthening intuition.

Fire is perhaps the Element most often associated with Witchcraft in the popular imagination. This could be because the spirit of fire is so easy to observe, as flames appear to dance on the wick or in the hearth. Candles are widely used in ritual, and often are a key part of magical work. Outdoor rituals may make use of bonfires, which become very powerful tools of transformation. Burning a small piece of paper with intentions written on it is often an effective way to "seal" magical work.

In the next section, we'll get more acquainted with each of the Elements, taking a look at their characteristics, magical associations, and effects on our lives. We'll also look at how the Fifth Element— Spirit—works through each of the other four, and by extension, through ourselves.

PART TWO

ELEMENTAL PHILOSOPHY

THE ELEMENTS

There are many different ways to view the Elements and their significance to Wicca and Witchcraft.

First, let's look briefly at the origins of this concept and its influence on contemporary practices, and then explore the Elements individually as physical and spiritual phenomena.

Understanding as much as you can about how each Element influences the human psyche, as well as the wider world, can help you deepen your magical relationships with these essential forces.

THE FOUR CLASSICAL ELEMENTS

The ancient Greeks believed that all matter was made up of one or more of four elements: Earth, Water, Air, and Fire. These were the basic building blocks of life, and nothing physical existed outside of them.

This idea persisted in scientific thought until a few centuries ago, and historians credit it with evolving into the discovery of the chemical elements modern scientists work with today. But the basic idea behind the Classical Elements, as the Greek concept is now called, was not just philosophy or physical science—the Elements also informed the Greeks' medical practices and spiritual traditions.

Of course, the Greeks were not alone—the notion of all things arising from a handful of natural phenomena is also found in ancient Egypt and Babylonia, and forms of the concept exist in Hinduism, Buddhism, and religions within China and Japan.

Eastern systems differ in the number and identification of Elements. Chinese astrology, for example, recognizes Fire, Water, and Earth, leaving out Air, but includes the two key substances of Wood and Metal, which fall under Earth in Western traditions. The Chinese did not view these Elements as different fixed substances, but more as different forms of energy which is always in flux—an idea, as we have seen previously, echoed in much of the new scientific thinking about the basic nature of matter. Ancient Tibetan philosophy mirrors the original Greek system but adds Space as a fifth Element.

THE FIFTH ELEMENT

The Greeks themselves came to add a fifth Element in the form of what they called *aether*, a word that both names a primordial deity of air and translates as "pure air" or "clear sky." Aether was believed to embody the "upper air," or the air that the gods breathed in the celestial sphere. Among philosophers, Aether was long classified as a type of Air, but Aristotle determined it to be a distinct Element in and of itself, and added it to the list.

This Fifth Element is also widely called *Akasha*, from the Sanskrit word meaning "space." The concept of Akasha appears across many Eastern traditions and is described in one way or another as the original Element from which all creation came, and which still exists in everything and in limitless capacities outside of what we perceive to be the material world.

Later spiritual and religious philosophies would come to associate Akasha with the concept of "Spirit," which is how it is generally defined in Wiccan and Pagan circles.

The Fifth Element is the source and substance of all creation, the invisible unifying force of the Universe, and the conduit through which magic is affected. That it has so many different names and descriptions is perhaps due to its quality of being completely intangible and always mysterious.

ELEMENTAL RELATIONSHIPS

If we take a look at the role the Elements play in ensuring and sustaining life, it's not hard to see why they have been considered the fundamental building blocks of reality.

The human body can be seen as an illustration of this concept, as it makes use of Earth for fuel, Water for substance and sustenance (both in its pure Elemental form and in the form of the blood running through our veins), Fire for the digestive and reproductive processes, and Air for the breath that keeps everything moving. Each Element contributes to our survival, yet each can and does exist entirely independent of us, and of all living beings.

What's just as important as their existence as individual forces, however, is the way they combine and interact to produce the complexity of the world as we know it.

There are several manifestations of the co-creative and interdependent relationships between the Elements. Fire needs Earth and Air to exist, even as it can consume both. And yet, Air can extinguish Fire, depending on the amount and force of each. Water is both absorbed by Earth and able to shape and cover it. Water and Air share the ingredient of oxygen, and each can contain the other. The interrelated qualities of the Elements have powerful potential in spirituality and magic, as in all other areas of life.

THE ELEMENTS AND MODERN OCCULTISM

The influence of the concept of the Elements on Western cultures can be seen in many spiritual and esoteric practices.

While the tradition of alchemy is no longer the popular interest that it was in the Middle Ages, its foundation in the process of transformation using both physical and spiritual means was inspired by the Classical Elements, and has echoes in many modern Pagan traditions. A more widely contemporary Occult tradition with roots in the Middle Ages is the divination system known as the Tarot.

Once used as playing cards in 14th century Europe, Tarot decks grew to be adopted in later centuries as a spiritual tool for accessing information not available on the physical plane. Each card in the Tarot is associated with an Element. In the Minor Arcana, the Elements determined according to the four suits:

Suit	Element
Wands	Fire
Coins	Earth
Cups	Water
Swords	Air

Each suit has associated meanings that correlate to the properties of that Element, which can be used to gain insights into a given Tarot reading. For example, the cards in the suit of Air will pertain to issues of intellect and outlook, decision-making and mental struggles. Many Swords in a given reading may indicate that the questioner is struggling with a conflict or negative attitude, or simply needs to look more closely at a situation.

Undoubtedly though, astrology can take the most credit for keeping an awareness of the Elements alive in popular culture.

Each sign in the wheel of the Zodiac is associated with a specific Element, and astrology holds that our personal characters are shaped not only by the arrangement of the planets at the time of our birth, but also by the qualities of the Element associated with our Sun sign.

Scorpios, for example, tend to be strongly affected by emotions and introspective, though they can be outwardly quite direct and intense in their projection of energy. The other Water signs, Pisces and Cancer, are also more under the pull of their emotions than Earth or Air, but can be more compassionate than Scorpio in the way they relate to others. The Earth signs—Capricorn, Taurus and Virgo—are more grounded and practical than Water signs. Aquarius, Gemini, and Libra, associated with Air, are more detached and can seem unemotional, while Fire signs—Aries, Leo, and Sagittarius—tend toward enthusiasm and impatience.

ELEMENTS
AND PERSONALITIES

There's much to learn from the connection with astrology when it comes to how the Elements affect us as people.

While every person is a unique individual, and no two personalities will ever be exactly alike, some broad generalizations can be made about the dominant characteristics of people based on the Element associated with their Sun sign—their dominant Element. *Note, a Sun sign is also referred to as a Star sign or Zodiac sign.*

These characteristics include both positive and negative traits, and each Element comes with its own strengths and challenges. Knowing our dominant Element can help us see ourselves, our individual approaches to life, and our way of interacting with others from a more objective viewpoint. This can help us learn to balance the traits that are not useful in our lives.

If you don't know your Sun sign and thus don't know your Element, it's a good idea to find it by looking up your birthday on the wheel of the Zodiac, or in the table at the end of this book. As you read these introductions to the Elements, their fundamental qualities, and their implications for the human psyche, make note of what you recognize in yourself, as well as what you don't identify with.

You will likely resonate with your dominant Element, but most people find that qualities of other Elements describe them accurately as well. This is because our Sun signs are only one aspect of our makeup according to astrology. Knowing your Moon and Rising signs can offer additional insight into your personality from an Elemental point of view. For example, you might have all three signs in Fire, or have every Element but Earth represented.

Many people find that the Element(s) they're missing in terms of these three aspects of their birth chart corresponds to qualities they struggle to balance. If you seem *not* to be described at all by a particular Elemental description below, you may be missing that Element in your chart!

EARTH

The Element of Earth is probably the most obvious to human perception, since Earth is where we live.

Even those of us in highly urban areas without much access to natural environments are aware that underneath all that pavement is the Earth, without which we would have nowhere to build our houses, roads, and cities.

Earth is, literally, the ground we walk on, as well as where we raise the animals and grow the food we need to survive and thrive. It has also been the source of the clay and minerals with which we've made pottery and cookware to prepare and eat our food, and the trees and stone we've used to build our dwellings.

For the vast majority of human history, the Earth provided everything we needed to survive as a species, with very little in the way of the complex and environmentally damaging processes that go into manufacturing so many of our modern goods. As modern societies, we seem to hold an awareness of this seeming distance from our origins with phrases like "back to the Earth" or "back to the land," used to refer to a felt need to escape the busy, modern city life and spend time in nature.

The idea of being "grounded" is another common metaphor that speaks to the central role Earth plays in our lives. Whether it's a teenager being punished for staying out too late or a busy adult trying to shake off the distractions of the work day through meditation, there's a tradition in modern culture that emphasizes "keeping our feet on the ground" in order to navigate this life successfully. Earth is certainly the most "grounding" of the Elements, with its stable, heavy, passive energy and calming effect.

As a physical reality in and of itself, Earth mostly appears to be unmoving. As such, Earth is associated with the qualities of patience, endurance, and permanence. However, we do see movement in the animals that roam the Earth and, at somewhat slower paces, in the growth of plant life. This connection to growth brings the qualities of diligence and commitment, and the ability to reap what one sows.

Earth personalities

People with Earth as their dominant Element tend to be practically-minded, and are considered to be "sensible" by their peers.

Oriented to the physical manifestations of reality as we know it, Earth people tend to place emphasis on what can be proven through the experience of the five senses, rather than on more subtle, less easily-perceived phenomena. They tend to be reliable, productive, and disciplined, with an innate sense for the workings of the material world and a methodical approach to work that enables them to achieve material security with greater ease than other Elemental personalities. They value stable and long-term friendships and make for honest and kind friends.

The challenge for Earth people is to not let their practicality and desire for structure to keep them from discovering and reveling in life's mysteries, or accessing their own emotional states. Too much Earth energy can lead to becoming rigid or narrow-minded, actually limiting our potential for growth by closing ourselves off to higher-frequency energies that inspire us with new perspectives and motivate us to set our sights on new horizons. People who are described as being "stubborn as a rock" or behaving like "a stick in the mud" are probably exhibiting an excess of Earth energy, and would benefit from loosening up and allowing themselves more access to mystery and joy. They may not always realize that security is, like everything else, ultimately impermanent, that growth is cyclical, and that there are always unseen forces which we may not be able to control, but can make an effort to better understand.

Even the most sensible habits and patterns of living can become overly rigid, and without a certain amount of flexibility it can be hard to navigate the occasional interference that life throws our way. The Earth itself manifests the inevitability of disruption in the form of earthquakes, a phenomenon echoed in the phrase "shaken up" to describe how we feel when unexpected events wreak havoc on the seeming predictability of our daily lives. "Uprooted" is another Earth-related metaphor for how we experience moving from a place we've called home or changing jobs. We are, as human beings, oriented to the ground, and it can be difficult for those with Earth as their dominant energy to feel comfortable in the face of dynamic change.

Ways of connecting with Earth

The Element of Earth is physically represented by the land itself, and all natural forms existing within it and on it.

Trees and forests, rocks and caves, fields and groves are all associated with Earth, and spending time in places that have one or more of these features is a great way to connect with the Earth Element.

Plunge your hands into fresh soil in a garden, walk barefoot in the mud or the grass, or climb a giant boulder and sit on it, feeling its energy resonate with yours. Lie down under the shelter of a leafy tree and feel the ground beneath you supporting your weight, keeping you stable and secure. Place the palm of your hand gently against the trunk of the tree and hold it there for a few moments. Notice its calming effect on your body and thank the tree for its nourishing and sheltering existence.

If you can't get outside, you can practice attuning to Earth energy with a single house plant. Gently touch the soil and the leaves and thank the plant for keeping you company. Spend time noticing and appreciating of the Earth's bounty that you bring home from the grocery store. Hold a potato or other root vegetable in your hands and smell the earthy scents. Doing this before preparing a meal can add much love, intention, and quality to your dinner! Be sure not to take Earth for granted, as it is the foundation of your existence and the ultimate source of all of your abundance.

AIR

In contrast to the visibility of Earth, Air is the Element that we cannot really see at all.

We experience it mostly through our tactile and audial senses, feeling the strength and temperature of a breeze, or hearing the howl of the wind during a storm. Of course, we are in constant interaction with Air via the breath, even though most of the time we're not conscious of it. In fact, you might say Air is the Element we notice the least, unless and until we don't have enough of it!

Air is a traveling energy, not limited to the ground-level perspective of Earth inhabitants, but free to rise and move over great distances. Air inhabits vast realms we have no access to, though recently we've been able to glimpse Air's domain via planes, helicopters, and space shuttles. Because its light density renders it relatively "immune" to gravity, the energy of Air is detached and instantly changeable. Though its quality can be tempered by the presence of the other Elements, Air cannot ever be truly contained.

Air carries sounds and scents from nearby locations, and so informs us about our surrounding environments. We also communicate by pushing air through the lungs and throat in order to speak or sing. Air energy is therefore associated with the qualities of intellect, mental clarity, and communication, and represents the source of knowledge and ideas. It is also the Element of imagination and inspiration—indeed, we speak both literally and figuratively of "needing fresh air" when our indoor environments, or our lives, have become stagnant. We also talk of surprises as coming "out of thin air" or "out of the blue," as if to recognize the link between the invisible forces that influence our lives and the air itself.

Air personalities

People with Air personalities tend to enjoy a higher degree of emotional detachment and objectivity than those with other dominant Elements.

Their "bird's eye view" on life can help them see patterns and possibilities that others can't, and thus avoid the pitfalls of shortsightedness or "stuckness" that people with other personalities might struggle with. Air people tend to have very active minds and feel at home in the realms of abstract thought. They have a knack for discovering new ideas. They are socially energetic and take an interest in the ideas of others, but their dynamic nature and need for movement and free expression may keep them from hanging around in one place for any length of time. They don't want to miss anything by being away too long from their regular, broad-perspectived perch.

The challenge for Air people, then, is to balance their flightiest, high-level energies with more grounded, fixed energies, or else all of that intellectual potential may stay unmanifested in the material world. Just as having one's "feet on the ground" is considered a positive attribute, we tend to speak of having one's "head in the clouds" as something to avoid, at least for too much of the time. "Flighty" is another descriptive word with less-than-positive connotations to describe people who seem to lack focus or substance. Air people need to learn to appreciate the value in being still, as well as being in touch with their emotions, which can often be an uncomfortable realm for them. Getting regular exercise can help them move some of that mental energy to the rest of the body, creating a balance that allows those Air qualities to manifest in more grounded ways.

Ways of connecting with Air

The simplest, most instantly available method for attuning to the energies of Air is through conscious attention to our breath. There are many different meditative breathing exercises, practiced in a range of spiritual and healing traditions, that are worth exploring for their many health benefits. But you can also simply sit with your eyes closed and notice how it feels to breathe.

Another way to spend some time with Air is to watch how individual leaves on a tree interact with the breeze. Anyone who has paid attention knows that leaves and branches don't all move uniformly in response to the push of wind—although in particularly strong winds, this may appear to be the case. Most of the time, if you watch closely, some branches will bend lower than others, and some leaves will flip and flutter much more vigorously than others. Observed in this way, the unpredictable intricacies of Air's movements can be fascinating.

Simply focusing your attention on how Air feels on your skin can be reenergizing, particularly on a hot day when a cool breeze comes sweeping in, even for just a moment. Burning incense is another potential way to bring the positive qualities of Air into your awareness. If you're lucky enough to live in an area that offers views from high elevations, spending some time in such places is great for refreshing your perspective. Mountain locations are ideal for this kind of communing with the Air Element, but rooftops, particularly on tall buildings, can also work wonders. Finally, resurrect that childhood habit of looking for shapes in the passing clouds. (If you never did that as a child, make up for it by starting now!) Notice the pace at which the clouds are moving, whether crawling or racing across the sky, and how their shapes are in constant flux, even when they appear to be relatively still. Cloud-gazing can, with practice and intention, become a powerful method of divination for those able and willing to receive information in this way.

Even when the wind blows hard enough to cause inconvenience, and even though temperatures may be too hot or cold for your liking, be sure to appreciate and thank the Element of Air for its effortless availability in sustaining your life.

FIRE

Fire is probably the most attention-grabbing of all the Elements, due as much to its mesmerizing appearance as to its inherent dangers.

While early humans did live without the use of fire for millennia, the discovery of how to create and control it was essential to our evolution as a species. Fire has allowed us to work and play after sundown, cook nutritious meals, and live comfortably in colder climates. Though its ability to consume nearly everything in its reach makes it a potentially deadly Element, it is this quality that also turns raw metals into tools for easier living.

Fire is different from the other Elements in that it must have another Element to consume in order to maintain its existence, and so is constantly at the work of transformation, and always in motion. It is also the Element of illumination, both for its ability to shed light in the dark, and its association with the Sun.

The energy of Fire is associated with passion—physical and spiritual—as well as strength, willpower, courage, and initiative. We see this demonstrated in the phrase "on fire," used often in amorous contexts, as well as being "fired up" about something one feels to be important, whether a political opinion or a sports team. We also might speak of "feeling the heat" of a stressful or pressurized situation or "putting the heat on" someone in order to get something we want. Fire is also associated with creativity, an energy that lights us up from the inside, as well as the ego, which we sometimes need to watch in order to not let our own thinking get out of control. It is the most active and animated of the Elements, and its power is something we all need to learn to recognize at an early point in our lives, lest we get burned for playing with it.

Fire personalities

People with Fire as their dominant Element tend to command the attention of others. They are generally enthusiastic, vigorous, impassioned, and easily excitable. They make for natural leaders, since they are naturally courageous and willing to charge forth, and they often feel passionate enough about causes or goals that nothing gets in the way of their drive to succeed.

Others are drawn to the light Fire people radiate from the center of their beings. They are often joyful people, and others may feel "lighter" just for being around them. Fire people don't tire easily and tend not to be comfortable sitting still for very long. This is energy that can't be truly contained without extinguishing it.

Of course, just as the Element can be dangerous when not carefully managed, the personality of Fire can get to be too much for others. Fire people may sometimes go overboard in expressing their desires or opinions, or be unaware of the need to "share the floor" during conversations. They can be impulsive and somewhat insensitive compared to other Elemental personalities. They may struggle with a perceived need for immediate gratification or have the tendency to be in a hurry all the time. Too much Fire energy can make a person quick-tempered or even prone to rage, and courage untempered by reason and realism can end up *backfiring*—another word that demonstrates our appreciation for the power of fire.

A balanced approach to living as a Fire person involves learning to ease up on the fuel when appropriate, taking a more long-range view of what will be needed to sustain that energy beyond the present moment. In the days before electricity, households would "bank" their indoor fire overnight, allowing the embers to stay just hot enough to keep it intact for the next morning. Fire people can remember that slowing down and cooling off does not have to mean being extinguished, but can instead be a wise way to ensure success in the long run.

Ways of connecting with Fire

Fire is the one Element that we can't touch with our bodies without potentially serious damage, including death.

Therefore, attuning to its energy is, in the most immediate sense, a "hands-off" activity. However, interacting with Fire is intense, illuminating, and exhilarating all the same, and one can be just as immersed in its energy as in any of the other Elements. Gazing into the flame of a candle is a wonderful, simple way to take in the power of Fire, and a bonfire is even better, especially on a cool, crisp evening when the warmth of the fire adds an extra layer to its magical quality. A fire enjoyed by friends, families, and/or lovers is one manifestation of the love energy this Element brings, as well as its ability to strengthen bonds with others.

Like clouds, flames can make for excellent divinatory communication, as images may appear either in the fire itself, or the smoke as it twists and curls up toward the sky. Crackling embers and the small bursts of energy they release can also be interpreted as messages from the spirit world, and there are even several methods for divination using the ashes from ritual fires.

Moving the body with vigorous exercise and dance is another way to tap into Fire, stoking the heat of our internal "engines" to match the high frequency and vitality of this Element. This way of attuning has the added benefits of building up strength and clearing toxins and other unwanted energy forms from the body. Spending time outdoors in the Sun is also important, and can be extra magical after a long spell of rain or cold Winter weather. Even though the Sun is technically composed of gas, rather than Fire, the two have always been linked together. After all, the Sun does have the ability to burn our skin, and it can certainly start a fire under the right circumstances!

In many traditions, blowing out a candle is considered disrespectful to the spirit of Fire, and people will wave their hands over the flame to put it out instead, or use candle snuffers as a gentler, more attentive method. Whether you adhere to this idea or not, always be respectful of and grateful for the gift of Fire.

WATER

Water shares with Air the ability to move easily, and is the shape-shifter of the Elements. Also like Air, it inhabits physical realms we can't access, in the form of the deepest depths of the oceans and the glacier-covered extremes of the North and South poles.

Water covers most of the planet and manifests in a dizzying array of forms, from the smallest raindrop to an unfathomable tsunami. Essential to the makeup and survival of all living things, Water is nourishing and often soothing, provided we're not tumbling in the rough surf of the ocean or getting drenched in a torrential rain storm!

Water can be completely still or in constant motion, can appear to disappear completely as it joins with Air, and can change to solid form. Its ability to exist in three different states of matter is a testament to the mutability and flexibility of Water. Water will always take the shape of whatever contains it, be it a cup, a pipe, or a depression in a rock. Indeed, it always follows the path of least resistance, as seen when rivers create new pathways in the Earth to get around physical obstacles. Water is powerful—it can flood dry land, extinguish Fire, and when combined with Air can it even dissolve metal over time—but it is also cleansing and purifying.

Water's ability to flow connects it to the realm of human emotions, demonstrated most physically by tears of sadness and joy. The phrase "welling up" is sometimes used to describe a sudden onset of tears caused by emotion. Water is also associated with psychic abilities, as is the Moon, which links to Water through the push and pull of ocean tides. Sensitivity and intuition are related qualities of Water, as are romanticism, generosity, and empathy.

Water personalities

People with Water as a dominant Element are the most naturally psychic of all the Elemental personalities.

Even if they don't realize the source of their intuition and intense feeling, they can be incredibly sensitive to the moods and energies of others, whether those people are in the same room, or, in the case of those they're emotionally close to, very far away on the physical plane.

Water people tend to have a deep understanding of the makeup and motives of the human psyche, and make for good healers and listeners. They are generally creative types, with mystical leanings and an appreciation for the sensual. The energy of Water allows them to be more at home in their emotions than others, which is essentially a prerequisite to being an artist of any kind. Water people love to be in love, and are immersed in the connections they form with others.

The challenges of carrying Water energy include intense emotionality and difficulty maintaining psychic boundaries.

Water people can be overly sensitive, to the point that they are essentially immobilized by all of the stimuli around them and risk drowning in other people's emotions and energies. Depression can be a recurring issue for Water people, as can obsession with wanting to know the unknown before such knowing is possible. Indeed, a drawback of the high levels of psychic activity in Water is that they get accustomed to accessing information unavailable through the usual five senses, and they can get stuck seeking answers to questions they just aren't meant to have answered at the time. They may also unintentionally give away too much of their power to negative people who feed off their kindness and loving natures, and thus become drains on the energies of others.

Some natural Water bodies are stagnant, which, while beneficial for some life forms, is unhealthy for humans to drink. Likewise, Water people can succumb to laziness and lethargy if their energy frequencies are too low. Earth energy is a good starting point for Water people who need balance, as the ground can absorb excess Water. Fire, Water's opposite, can shed light into the shadows, raise the frequency, and brighten the mood.

Ways of connecting with Water

Probably the most powerful way to attune to the energies of Water is to immerse yourself in it.

Swimming in any natural body—ocean, lake, river or pond—is an ideal experience of communion with nature, but this can be a far-away or even unattainable luxury for many people. A pool can also do the trick, as can a relaxing soak in the bathtub. The next time you're immersed in Water, notice the feel of it on your skin and the difference in the way it feels to move your body.

Of course, it isn't strictly necessary to be completely immersed in Water to be in tune with its energy. Dipping a toe or a foot into a stream, taking a refreshing shower, or even running your hand through a bowl of water also forms a direct connection, as does appreciating a long, cold drink of water to quench a thirst.

Water is also experienced through sight and sound—walking along a river or spending time on the beach gazing out at the waves is calming to the body, as is the sound of rain or small waves quietly lapping a shoreline or a river bank. Even recordings of water sounds can help bring people more in touch with their inner selves! As mentioned previously, the calm surface of a bowl of water or even a pond or lake can be used for scrying—Water can speak to you through images, just like clouds and fire. Wherever you encounter Water, be in gratitude for its healing, cleansing, purifying, and nourishing qualities. Allow it to help you open up to the unseen and mysterious forces at work in the Universe—both in yourself and in those around you.

ELEMENTS
AND THE OCCULT

While the Elements are found throughout the natural world, it is not *only* natural features, such as ponds or trees, that represent them in Wiccan and other pagan belief systems.

Ancient cosmologies often held particular gods and goddesses to be associated with one or more of the Elements (such as Vulcan, the Roman god of Fire, from whose name we get "volcano"), and Wicca has continued that tradition.

Other, "lesser" beings are also believed to inhabit the Elements, and these are seen in folklore from across the globe. Some of these entities are less suitable for a Witch's purposes than others—goblins, for example, are generally thought to be mischievous and ill-willed, while other Earth spirits, such as the Greek dryads, are of a more positive persuasion.

Finally, each Element has many associated animals that embody the spirit energy of Earth, Air, Fire, and Water. Wiccans and other Witches may work with deities, Elemental beings, and/or animals as representations of the Elements in their individual spiritual practices.

ELEMENTS AND DEITIES

For those whose belief systems include specific deities, there are many gods and goddesses from cultures around the world who are associated with individual Elements.

Working with these deities in ritual and magic can strengthen your alignment with the Elements, whether you are focusing specifically on magic associated with one particular Element or all of them. It's worth doing some research to discover deities who resonate with you personally, by reading the myths and stories around them and connecting with the cultures they originate in, but here are a few brief examples.

Earth deities include the Greek goddess Demeter, also known as Ceres in the Roman cosmology. She is the goddess of fertility and agriculture, specifically of crops that are processed into edible grains. In fact, the name "Ceres" is the root of the word "cereal," which demonstrates how our modern culture is still connected to ancient beliefs. Ceres was often depicted with a garland of wheat and a basket of fruit and flowers. The god Cernunnos, worshipped throughout Celtic Europe, is also associated with Earth. He is the god of animals, as well as forests and vegetation, and is seen in Paleolithic cave paintings in the form of a stag. He is considered the oldest of the gods in the Celtic pantheon, born of the original mother goddess.

The Egyptian Nut (pronounced "Noot") was the goddess of the sky and the heavens, and so she makes for a good deity to work with in Air magic. Her name is often translated to mean "sky," and, like Cernunnos, she is also a very old deity, found in the creation story of the ancient city of Heliopolis. She was often rendered as a blue-skinned, star-covered woman, arching over the Earth on hands and feet. The widely-known god Thoth is also often associated with Air, as he is credited with inventing writing in the form of hieroglyphs, as well as magic, science, astronomy, and a host of other intellectual pursuits.

In the realm of Fire, the Greek Prometheus plays a crucial role in the origins and development of humankind. He was tasked by Zeus to create the first man from Water and Earth, and then of his own accord he gave humans the power of Fire by stealing it from Zeus' lightning. Brigid, a central figure in the Celtic pantheon and the Irish pantheon in particular, is associated with Fire as the goddess of healing and smithcraft—the art of forging metal over flame. She is said to rule over the "fires" of inspiration, the forge, and the hearth, and sacred flames were kept continually burning in her honor, in some places into the 13th century.

Because the Element of Water is fluid and shape-shifting, existing in such a wide variety of forms, straightforward associations between Water and particular deities are a little more difficult to identify. Many "lesser" deities are associated with specific locations such as rivers and springs, and some of the crone goddesses and underworld gods have Water associations, but deities specifically linked to the Element of Water don't appear with as much frequency as those of the other Elements.

Nonetheless, we still find a pair of ancient Sumerian deities—Enki and Nammu—credited with the origins of the world through their associations with Water. Nammu was the goddess of the primordial sea who gave birth to heaven and earth. Enki, born from the air and the earth, was the god of groundwater, or the "freshwater sea" that Sumerians believed existed under the Earth, and was said to have first filled the empty riverbeds with water.

These are just a few examples of deities you might seek relationships with in your exploration of the Elements. They are given in gender pairs to show possibilities for incorporating both female and male deities—the Goddess and God of the Old Religion—with an emphasis on one or more Elements.

You may feel called by a particular goddess or god, or even by a particular Element—if so, that's a definite sign that you would benefit from pursuing spiritual study in that direction. As always, you should follow your own path and go with your own instincts.

ELEMENTAL BEINGS

Many Pagan and Wiccan traditions also believe in what are usually called "Elementals," or "Elemental Beings."

These are the spirits of Earth, Air, Fire, and Water, and they harken back to the animistic world view of the ancients. These spirits have many names, take many forms, and are the subjects of centuries of legend and lore. Wiccans and Witches who work with Elementals will attest to their presence in nature and in magical ritual.

These beings are said mostly to be unseen, although some particularly sensitive people have seen glimpses of them. Keeping an open mind and a willingness to learn and discover can help you learn to contact and sense them, and ask for their help in your magical workings.

Earth Elementals are widely identified as "gnomes" (meaning "Earth dwellers") in the Western world, although they are also known as "elves," "trolls," and even "faeries." (Some consider faeries to be Air Elementals, but others, such as the Irish, refer to the spirits of the Earth as faeries.)

These spirits can inhabit a variety of natural features in a given landscape, but are most commonly associated with wooded areas, rocks, caves, and earthen mounds. Spending time in a quiet, undisturbed outdoor area is a good way to start working to connect with Earth spirits. Because of Earth's connection with prosperity and material abundance, leaving offerings like sparkling stones can encourage a relationship with these spirits to flourish.

Working with Earth Elementals in magic is appropriate for spells related to prosperity and success, as well as helping balance negative tendencies toward manipulation and greed. Earth spirits are also helpful in instilling the basic tenacity required to build gradual and long-term abundance, by increasing confidence, practicality, and consistency, as well as a more skillful balance of ambition, caution, and patience.

Air Elementals are most commonly referred to as "sylphs," but, as mentioned above, may also be likened to winged faeries.

They are considered to be present in the clouds, in blowing wind, and other weather phenomena like heavy storms of rain or snow, and were believed in ancient cultures to bring divinatory messages to those able to listen. These spirits of Air are light in energy and quick-moving, so connections with them may have a more fleeting quality than those with Earth spirits, but they also may be felt more tangibly.

It's easier to commune with Air spirits on a breezy or windy day than in very still conditions, but, being of the Air, they are all around us nonetheless. Whistling and/or singing can help one attune with Air Elementals, as can paying attention to any flying insects in the vicinity. It also helps to leave offerings of flowers, which these spirits are said to love.

In magic, Air spirits are helpful for work involving the intellect and communication, developing finer sensitivities to the invisible realms, and responding skillfully to change. As they are also associated with music, they can be called upon to help harmonize disruptive circumstances or relationships.

Fire Elementals are known as "salamanders," perhaps because to those who can perceive them visually: they look like small lizards with tongues of flame, although others see them as tiny balls of light.

These spirits live in all forms of flame, lightning, and the heat of the Sun, and are said to be the catalysts that make the existence of Fire possible.

They are considered by many to be the most powerful of the Elemental beings, and can be fairly easily summoned with the lighting of a candle or building of a fire. Burning incense or sage is a good way to honor and thank them for their presence.

Fire spirits can aid in transformative magic, helping us to see what needs to be eliminated from our lives in order to make room for new growth. Spells for courage, passion, and extra energy are in Fire's domain, both on physical and spiritual levels. Just as the physical manifestation of Fire is potentially dangerous, it's important to respect the power of the spirits of Fire, and not be reckless or excessive with their energies.

Water Elementals are most commonly referred to as "undines," but have also been represented as water nymphs and mermaids in Western traditions.

Existing in all forms of water, these spirits are most commonly associated with rivers, lakes, oceans, springs, wells, and waterfalls.

Spending time near a natural body of water is the most ideal way to connect with Water spirits, who may acknowledge your presence with bubbles or subtle ripples in an otherwise calm surface. Rainy days can also be good occasions for communing with these Elementals. Of course, you can also gaze into the water in a bowl or cauldron.

They are said to appreciate essential oils as offerings, but be sparing with any substance you pour into a natural body of water, and be sure that it's entirely nontoxic to any marine life.

Water spirits are helpful in magic related to love, creativity, and healing, as well as balancing extreme emotions. They help us get in touch with our inner feelings and become more flexible in our approach to solving problems.

People who are new to the Craft sometimes have difficulty taking the concept of Elemental beings seriously.

This is partly due to the way Elementals have been portrayed in our modern, commercialized culture, via Disney movies and Halloween costumes, but it may also be that these spirits are simply not part of one's individual experience of nature. Whether or not you perceive the energies of the Elements as having distinct names and forms, musing on these legendary beings can provide a way into a deeper relationship with the Elements themselves.

As you put more intention into your observance of the natural world, they may just show up for you—as the appearance of faces in trees, a sudden breeze, or dancing shadows around the fire.

ANIMALS AND THE ELEMENTS

Of course, there is another kind of "Elemental being" which is far more tangible on our plane of existence: every living creature in the animal kingdom. Animals have played important roles in myth, legend, and spirituality in traditions throughout the world, and are considered sacred by many Witches and Wiccans.

Some Witches work with animal "familiars," which may be physical creatures actually living in their environments, or psychic connections with one or more animals on a purely spiritual level. Others may discover and work with what they describe as "power" or "totem" animals, borrowing from Native American and other shamanic traditions.

In many Wiccan traditions, each of the Elements is associated with a variety of specific animals. Usually, these correspondences relate to habitat—so that most birds are considered Air animals, most sea creatures are Water animals, etc. But habitat is only one source of association. Myths, legends, and characteristics of the animal in question also come into play, particularly when it comes to the animals of Fire.

For example, the lion has long been associated with solar deities, and embodies the qualities of strength, courage, and intensity. Therefore, the lion belongs to the Element of Fire. So does the red fox, associated with passion and desire, and known for its ability to think quickly and change course with agility. The praying mantis is another Fire animal, credited with creating fire among the San people of the Kalahari Desert. The mantis' capacity for both stillness and swift, destructive action is also a source of this association.

Earth animals include the wolf, known for its loyalty and generosity among its own kind; the bear, symbolizing both tranquility and great power; and even the ant, which uses its industrious and determined nature to build its home literally out of the Earth.

Two obvious Air animals are the raven, associated with eloquence and self-knowledge, and the hummingbird, which reminds us of the importance of agility and playfulness. A less obvious correspondence with Air is the spider, which does not fly but spends much of its time suspended above the ground, and is associated with divine inspiration.

Water animals include the dolphin, seen by the ancient Celts as "the watcher of the waters" and associated with playfulness and transcendence; the turtle, able to navigate both land and sea and so associated with adaptability as well as endurance; and the swan, seen as symbolic of grace and elegance.

Often, the sudden or recurring appearance of an animal in one's life is thought to be a message from the spirit world.

You don't have to be a Witch or a shaman for this to happen in your life. If a particular animal keeps crossing your path, whether literally or in the form of dreams or other seemingly significant references, it can be beneficial to do some research regarding the animal's esoteric meanings, including its associated Element.

You may be being asked to learn something new about yourself, or pay attention to an area of your life that you've been neglecting. As living, breathing embodiments of the Universal life force, animals have much in common with us, and much to teach us about the unseen realms of our magical existence.

REVISITING
THE FIFTH ELEMENT

Having looked closer at each of the Elements that formed the original Classical system and their relationship to many aspects of the Old Religion, it's important to take another look at the Fifth Element—Akasha, or Spirit.

Of course, Spirit is not like the other Elements: it is completely intangible. Unlike the other four, it doesn't exist in its own form separate from anything else.

In a way, Spirit is very much like the sixth sense, which is different from the five senses that are rooted in the physiological processes of the body and therefore not always recognized as a sense. Regardless of their invisibility, Witches know that both Spirit and the sixth sense are very real, and it is often said that the sixth sense is the channel through which Spirit communicates with us. The sixth sense is essential to magic, just as the Fifth Element is essential to all of existence.

Another way of understanding the relationship between Spirit and the four tangible Elements is to look at the sacred meanings of numbers.

Various systems of numerology, dating back to ancient times, recognize the inherent magical qualities of individual numbers and their significance to all of creation. Wiccan and other Pagan traditions clearly value certain numbers—such as three, as reflected in the various triple deities, and thirteen, considered by many to be the ideal number of members in a coven. Two is represented in the male and female deities and the honoring of the night and the day.

The number four is particularly well-represented in the Wiccan belief system. There are four solar holidays in the Wheel of the Year—the equinoxes and solstices—as well as four Earth festivals: Imbolc, Beltane, Lughnasa, and Samhain. There are four main seasons, and four cardinal directions, from which four winds blow. And there are also those four suits, with their corresponding Elements, in the Minor Arcana of the Tarot.

Furthermore, many Wiccan and Pagan traditions connect each of the four tangible Elements to one of the cardinal directions, aligning two sets of four in a beautiful symmetry. This correspondence is enacted in spiritual and magical ritual, as we will see in the next section of this guide.

The alignment of the tangible Elements with these other occurrences of four is one reason why it doesn't make sense to try to "squeeze in" Spirit as a phenomenon in the same category. Instead, Spirit is already in each of the four, as it is in everything we can experience with our six senses, and in everything beyond that.

But there's another aspect of the sacred meaning of numbers—specifically, the number four and the number five—that mirrors the function of the Elements as building blocks in the process of all creation.

In numerological symbolism, the number one represents that which is about to form or take shape—it's the initial idea, thought, inspiration that leads to manifestation, and represents the male aspect of creation. Two, building on one, is the stage of gestation, as the idea takes root and begins to grow. Two is the female aspect. Three is the synthesis of inspiration and growth, and represents the expression of the completed idea, while four is viewed as the physical manifestation—the bringing forth of the idea into material form. The four Elements, seen as the original building blocks of the material world, are the physical manifestations of the original mental energy that created what we know as the Universe.

The number five, then, is essentially what makes new creation possible. It is the necessary catalyst that stirs up the perfect symmetry of the four in order to keep the Universal energy moving—the force that keeps all of creation from being static instead of dynamic. The five is the conduit for manifesting what we desire through magical intention.

This number is represented in the pentacle, a major symbol in most Wiccan traditions. The star has five points—one for each tangible Element and one for Spirit. The circle that connects the points pulls all of creation together, and can be said to also represent Spirit, the source of all existence.

Spirit, as the Fifth Element, is what underlies the energy emitted by a crystal, the interaction of a plant with everything visible and invisible in its environment, and the response of water, at the molecular level, to the energies of particular emotions.

It infuses us as living beings, both when we are aware of it and when we are not. When we are aware of Spirit, and when we have clear, positive intentions, we can utilize this basic core energy to manifest desired change in the world. In the next section of this guide, we'll take a more in-depth look at how the magical properties of all five Elements can be channeled to do just that.

PART THREE

ELEMENTAL MAGIC

THE ELEMENTS IN WICCAN RITUAL

Ritual traditions vary widely, but most followers of the Craft involve the Elements on some level in their practice.

Usually, the Elements are invoked at the start of a ritual—whether it's one of the holidays on the Wheel of the Year, an Esbat (Full Moon celebration), or another occasion, such as an initiation into a coven or any other solitary event of a Witch's choosing.

The Elements are directly invited to participate in the ritual and are appreciated/thanked for their contributions. They may also be asked to assist in some kind of transformational working—a spell, a prayer, a sending of healing energies to a particular person or place. Involving the Elements is a way of connecting with the divine energy as it is expressed in these four distinct forms, allowing us to draw it forth from the incomprehensible source of All That Is into discernible channels.

TOOLS OF WITCHCRAFT

The Elements are usually represented physically on the altar by particular objects that symbolize their individual essences.

These objects are collectively referred to as "tools," though they can also be thought of as something like "ingredients" in the creation of something divine, positive, and timeless. There is quite a variety of tools in the world of Witchcraft, some more elaborate and/or difficult to obtain than others. Those covered here represent a fairly small handful of basic "ingredients" that are particularly relevant to the Elements.

First, a sacred space is necessary. Whether this is a permanent altar or shrine, a "dual-purpose" surface that doubles as a dresser or table, or even a space on the floor, the area where you place your tools and do your work needs to be deliberately chosen and dedicated to the purpose.

Next, you need something to represent each of the Elements. For Earth, a pentacle is great, but a bowl of salt or of earth itself works just as well. For Air, the traditional tool is the wand, which can be made very easily from a small tree branch. Some Witches like to use a bell or a feather instead. Water can be poured into a cup, bowl, or a small cauldron, if you happen to have one. (Alternatively, these can be left empty and still represent Water.) Although candles may be involved in the magical work itself and/or used as lighting, a tea light or other small candle can represent Fire on the altar. Some Witches use an athame, or ritual knife, for Fire.

An alternative is to use crystals or herbs to represent the Elements, which can be a simple and elegant way to connect with the natural world. Specific herbs and crystals associated with individual Elements can be found in the Tables of Correspondence at the end of this guide. If you don't have anything listed here for a particular Element, feel free to use and adapt what you have on hand—be creative! After all, whatever power particular objects may have, it's *you* that charges them, and it's your power fueling whatever transformation you seek.

That being said, it's important to realize that objects *do* have energy, as the animists have always known. Some will be much more energetically resonant than others, and some will feel more pleasant than others.

For example, think about some of your most treasured possessions—perhaps an heirloom passed down from a beloved relative or a work of art you created that you're pleased with. These objects have an energy in their own right, which is tied to how you feel about them, but exists on its own nonetheless.

The same is true of objects you don't feel positive about or attached to. Ever need to get rid of something that belonged to an old love? It's not just about the memories—it's the need to remove that physical energy from your life. Clearing out even your more mundane possessions just "feels good," not only because you've created more space, but because there's less *energetic* clutter, as well.

It is possible to clear an object from negative energy, but it's also true that some tools are just a better energetic fit for a particular person than others. So, again, choose what works best for you. Whatever objects you work with, however, it's important to clear them of all prior energetic imprints before using them in ritual and magic.

Clearing, or "cleansing" a tool can be done in several ways. If the object can get wet, you can start by rinsing it, or wiping it with a clean, dry cloth (it's best to keep a cloth or two just for this purpose, as opposed to something you use for regular housecleaning.) Following this, smudging with sage is a great way to clear energy, but you can also leave the object in sunlight or moonlight for a few hours, or bury it in sea salt, herbs, or soil. Go with your gut, or experiment with different methods to see what works best.

After clearing, it's time to charge the object with your own personal power and positive intention. Consecrating tools can be done with a simple ritual, with or without the more elaborate steps involved on other occasions. Some Witches choose to cast a circle and call the quarters first, while others consider consecration a separate step to be performed before a tool is ever placed on the altar.

Whichever you choose, you can charge the object by holding it over a candle flame (high enough not to burn it, of course!) and/or or lift it up toward the sky. You can also just hold it respectfully in your hands.

Verbalizing the consecration is highly recommended—the power of words goes a long way toward transforming energy, as we saw in the water crystal experiments we discussed in an earlier section. *What* to say is really very much up to you—many Witches prefer to use rhyme and rhythm in their spells, invocations, and other magical work, as this kind of language is considered particularly potent. Others choose their words in favor of being as precise as possible, whether they rhyme or not. You can also simply talk out loud about your intentions as you work to find your own magical voice.

Here's one suggestion for verbalizing the charging of tools:

"Through Earth, Air, Fire, Water and through Spirit, I consecrate this _____ to the Universe and all positive energy, to manifest my intentions with harm to none, and for the good of all."

This can be used with any object for all magical purposes, but if you wish to emphasize a symbolic representation with a particular Element, you might add a phrase or sentence declaring so. For example, *"I consecrate this wand to the Element of Air, and to the Universe..."*

SETTING UP YOUR ALTAR

As with everything else in Witchcraft, the way you set up your altar or sacred space is entirely up to you.

You should go with what feels right and what is visually pleasing for you—if it resonates with you, go with it. You might use a different set-up every time, or you might keep it the same for consistency. ("Ritual" does, after all, tend to involve following an established pattern.)

In terms of focusing on and working with the Elements, it's advisable to place your representations of each Element in its corresponding direction. This means your Earth symbol is in the North, or toward the top of the altar, your Air symbol is in the East (to the right), your Fire symbol is in the South (toward the bottom), and your Water symbol is in the West (to the left).

You may want something in the center to symbolize Spirit and its role in pulling together the other four Elements. This could be a candle, a quartz crystal, or some other object that is sacred to you.

CASTING THE CIRCLE

It is traditional in Wicca, as well as for other practitioners of the Craft, to cast a magic circle at the start of any ritual.

The circle serves as both a "container" inside which all of the magical energy you are raising will be concentrated, and a "protective boundary" that keeps out any unwanted energy—whether negative or just distracting.

Some Witches cast a circle every time they perform any ritual and/or magical act—even for consecrating tools. Others may save circle-casting for larger, more elaborate rituals such as those used in celebrating Sabbats and Esbats. Still others consider the circle completely optional, and may not cast one at all. This is an individual choice, but casting is recommended for beginners, as it can help you feel the energy you're raising in a more focused way.

There are many ways to cast a circle. You can physically mark the circle with candles, stones, herbs, and/or sea salt beforehand, or allow the circle to remain invisible. Standing inside the circle, point your wand, athame, or index finger to the ground at the circle's northernmost point. Walk clockwise around the circle, continuing to point, and visualize your personal power charging the ground at the circle's edge. You can do this just once, but it can be more effective to walk the circle three times, visualizing the power growing stronger with each rotation. Note: Make sure you have everything you'll need before you take this step, as it's not wise to break the energy of the circle once it's been cast!

CALLING THE QUARTERS

As mentioned above, each of the four Elements is associated with one of the four cardinal directions. When invoking the Elements into ritual, these directions, also called "quarters," serve as physical locations from which to locate and engage the specific energies of each Element.

Once the circle is cast (if you are doing so), the Elements can be invited into the sacred space. This can be a fairly simple step or a more elaborate process, depending on your preferences. Some Witches light a candle for each of the Elements while invoking them with words, and ritual hand gestures, while others may simply silently invite them into their ritual space.

Here is one approach to invoking the Elements that focuses on acknowledging the energetic identity of each. This can be done before any type of ritual, or as a way of starting your day by grounding and centering with the forces of nature. As you speak to each Element, be sure to face its corresponding direction.

Facing North:

Spirit of Earth,
Welcome to this sacred space.
Thank you for the gifts of stability and abundance,
and for bringing your energy to this moment.

Facing East:

Spirit of Air,
Welcome to this sacred space.
Thank you for the gifts of knowledge and harmony,
and for bringing your energy to this moment.

Facing South:

Spirit of Fire,
Welcome to this sacred space.
Thank you for the gifts of passion and transformation,
and for bringing your energy to this moment.

Facing West:

Spirit of Water,
Welcome to this sacred space.
Thank you for the gifts of intuition and empathy,
and for bringing your energy to this moment.

CLOSING THE RITUAL

Whatever your purpose for ritual—be it a Sabbat or a quick, simple spell—it's important to intentionally close the work and the sacred space before returning to "business as usual" in ordinary reality. (Neglecting to do so can result in feeling somewhat chaotic or "out of sorts," and possibly troubled sleep.)

Once your spiritual work is done, "release" the Elements by thanking them individually, perhaps moving in a counter-clockwise direction as you do so. If you have cast a circle, close it by walking counter-clockwise three times, visualizing any remaining magical energy returning to the ground. Stand quietly for a moment, clearing your mind of the ritual and/or spellwork, knowing that you've sent your power out into the Universe and that your intentions will be manifested in the way and at the time which is best for all.

MAGICAL PERCEPTION

Before we look at specific spells and other magical work, it's important to emphasize that simply following these steps as if following a recipe is unlikely to have any transformational effect.

The focused power of the mind is really where the magic comes from. This can be a challenge for many in this busy, noisy modern world, but developing some kind of meditation practice can strengthen your connection to the divine, and consequently, your magic.

There are many helpful resources out there in this department, including meditations, visualizations, and other mental/spiritual exercises specifically for the practice of Witchcraft. Below are four ways of strengthening your psychic "muscles" for magical work as you deepen your connection with the Elements.

EARTH: TALKING TO THE PHYSICAL WORLD

As you get up to start your day, and when you return from being out, say hello to your home. Say hello to each room, and to your favorite things in your home, whatever they may be.

This may feel a bit silly at first, but remember that there is Spirit in all things. As you get in the habit of greeting the energy in your home, you will notice that your mood lifts as you do so.

Pay extra attention to your magical and sacred objects—your altar tools, special stones, herbs, etc. Acknowledge the spirit energy in these objects, and thank them for being in your life. You are strengthening an energetic bond between you and these sacred tools that will empower your magical work.

AIR: BREATHWORK AND VISUALIZATION

A very effective way to ground and center before working magic is through conscious breathing. Through the breath we can open ourselves more deeply to the Element of Spirit and clear a path for sending our focused intentions out into the Universe. Basic 3-part yogic breathing is an ancient practice that quiets the mind and gets you closer to the state of mind that magical transformation requires.

Lying on your back, focus on breathing in slowly, allowing the air to fill your lower abdomen, then upper abdomen, then all the way to the top of your lungs. When it's time to breathe out, do so in the reverse order, pushing the air from the top of your body out first, and ending with the lower abdomen. (Note: It's best to breathe in and out through your nose, but if you have a cold, don't let that stop you!)

Do this five times, focusing entirely on your breath. Then, allow yourself to breathe normally, as you visualize the result of your intentions manifesting. For example, if you're dealing with money issues, call up the feeling of being completely secure in your finances, with all the bills paid and plenty to spare. Spend some time strengthening this feeling, and hold it as consistently as you can while you perform the magical work.

FIRE: FLAME AND FOCUS

Candles are great for strengthening concentration and psychic power. All you need is a quiet space and a lit candle.

For the first exercise, sit before the flame and gaze into it for a few moments. (Take care of your eyes by training your gaze toward the bottom of the flame, and be sure to blink whenever you need to.) When you're ready, close your eyes, and watch for the image of the flame against your closed eyelids. Hold onto this image for as long as you can before your concentration breaks. When the flame disappears, open your eyes and start again. Over time, you will be able to prolong the flame's appearance in your mind's eye.

Next, practice "shaping" the flame with your own thoughts. As you watch the flame, visualize it growing, shrinking, getting brighter and dimmer. Keep your focus trained on the flame and the change you're visualizing at the same time. You may not see an effect at first, as this takes practice, but after a time you will notice the flame respond to your projections. To strengthen the psychic energy further, be sure you've spoken to your candle and have done some meditative breathing first!

WATER: TRUSTING THE FLOW

This visualization is good for attaining an optimal mind frame for magic. Start with some meditative breathing. With eyes closed, bring to the "screen" of your mind an image of a pond. The surface of the pond is completely still, reflecting the blue sky above it and the tops of several tall trees around its perimeter.

You are standing at its southern shore, feeling the warmth of the Sun on your shoulders. Across the pond, to the North is a particularly large, knotty oak tree. To the East are three robins chattering to each other on the branches of a leafy shrub, and to the West, a stand of cattails and other marsh grasses obscure the pond's shoreline.

Hold this vision in your mind until it's quite solid. Then, visualize a small, round pebble in the palm of your dominant hand. Feel the smooth, cool surface of the pebble between your fingers, and then gently toss it into the center of the pond. Watch and hear the tiny splash it makes before disappearing under the surface. Watch the ripples it creates radiating out from the center in perfect circles. Choose a single small wave to focus on, following it until it travels all the way to the pond's northern shore.

Note how the ripples continue to move outward from the center, long after the pebble has settled on the bottom of the pond. This is a good metaphor for magic—the energy of the action continues to change the physical world around it long after the action itself has been performed.

ELEMENTAL SPELLS AND CHARMS

The following magical workings make use of the energies of the particular Element they are based in. These can be done as part of a larger ritual, or on their own. Be sure to ground and center beforehand, spending time in meditation and focusing on your intention.

Remember to always respect the power of magic, and do your work in the spirit of what is good for all and harms none.

Please note that while the ingredients listed below work well, you are free to make substitutions where necessary or desired. The Tables of Correspondence at the end of this guide provide more information about herbs, oils, and crystals in terms of their Elemental associations, and can be a starting place for finding alternatives.

EARTH SPELLS

Abundance Coins

This is a good charm for attracting extra money from unexpected places.

You will need:

- 2 coins—matching denominations of your choosing (older coins are nice if you have them, but it doesn't matter.)

- 1 small piece of cloth—a scrap of fabric is fine.

- 1 green ribbon

- 1 tablespoon total dried rosemary, thyme, and/or cinnamon

- Patchouli oil

Instructions:

Lay the herbs on the center of the cloth. Anoint the coins with a drop of the patchouli oil, speaking your intentions aloud as you do so—remember, your words are not particularly important, but rather the intent behind them.

Push the coins gently into the herbs, wrap the cloth over the coins, and tie with the ribbon. Place the coin bundle somewhere in your home where you will see it often, and carry it with you in your pocket or purse when you go out.

Harmony in the Home

To help with interpersonal conflicts or simply unsettled energy where you live, try this spell, which is particularly helpful in the weeks before Winter sets in.

You will need:

- Basil and honeysuckle, roughly one tablespoon of each—fresh herbs are preferable, but dried also works well.

- 1 dried leaf—if you must pick a leaf from a tree, choose from a well-flourishing tree, pick gently, thanking the tree, and leave the leaf to dry before using.

- Mortar and pestle—if you don't have these, a bowl and your fingertips will work fine.

- Cedar or sandalwood incense (optional)

Instructions:

Light the incense, if using. Slowly pour the basil into the mortar or bowl, saying, *"with this basil, I keep all negative energy away from my home."* Add the honeysuckle, saying, *"with this honeysuckle, I bring all positive energy into my home."* Stir the two herbs together with the pestle or mix with your fingertips. Take the leaf and crumble it gently over the herbs, saying, *"there is harmony in every corner of this home"* three times. Mix the leaf into the herbs while concentrating on feeling peaceful, at ease, and secure in your dwelling.

Sprinkle the mixture around the outside of your home, walking around it in a clockwise circle. If this is not possible, sprinkle it discreetly around as much of the outside area as you can. You can also use potted plants for this step, if necessary.

AIR SPELLS

Four Winds Incantations

The specific direction of the wind can make for an excellent magical tool, depending on your purposes. Try this on a particularly windy day for a stronger connection with the magical energy you're communing with. Be sure to choose an intention aligned with the wind's direction.

- North winds: financial, home, practical matters

- East winds: change, new beginnings, fresh perspective, creativity

- South winds: love, lust, passion, vitality, initiative, courage to follow through

- West winds: healing, cleansing, intuition, emotional concerns

Stand outdoors, facing the wind, with your feet a few inches apart, back straight, head held high, and arms a few inches from your sides with palms outward. (This is a slight modification the yogic "Mountain pose," appropriate here for its aid in aligning your vertical energy from the ground through the crown of your head. Mountains are also associated with the Element of Air.)

Take three deep breaths, place your palms together, and raise your arms to the sky. Verbalize your intention in connection with the wind. You might say, for example, "*In this East wind, I manifest a new way forward in my career, for the good of all, and with harm to none.*" Allow your intention to be carried on the wind. Then, keeping your palms together, slowly bring your hands down in front of your solar plexus. Take another deep breath, and close the ritual in your own way.

Spell for Clarity and Concentration

This is good for tests, projects at work, or anything that requires focus and feels challenging.

You will need:

- 1 dried dandelion flower (or leaf, if out of season)

- Peppermint oil

- 1 piece of paper

Instructions:

Write the task you're seeking help with on a piece of paper. Rub a drop of the peppermint oil into the paper as you say these words: "*With a sharp, clear, focused mind, I complete this well, in the desired time.*" Scatter the dandelion flowers/leaves over the paper, and leave it on your altar until the task is finished.

FIRE SPELLS

Transforming Through Banishing Old Habits

This spell enacts transformative magic through the physical burning of the representation of what you want to be rid of in your life—whether this is a physical habit or a way of thinking that you want to release.

You will need:

- 1 small black candle

- 1 small piece of paper

- 1 Fire-proof dish (or sink)

Instructions:

Light the candle. On the paper, either write or draw a symbol of what you are banishing. As you do so, imagine your life without this negative habit, and visualize the joy you will feel when it's gone. When you're ready, say, "*I release this habit of_____, and welcome in the positive energy created by its absence.*" Light the paper with the candle and let it burn out in the fire-proof dish, or in the sink, if necessary. (As with anything fire-related, be very careful with this step!) Leave the candle to burn out on its own in a safe place.

Bringing Love

This can be used to attract love into your life if you're single, or rejuvenate an existing relationship. However, if you struggle with self-love, your best bet is to start there, as you need it to sustain lasting love with someone else. Be very careful not to aim your energy at a specific person in a manipulative way, as this can backfire. In your visualization, you don't concentrate on controlling the feelings of another—instead, concentrate on how *you* want to feel.

You will need:

- 3 pink candles

- 1 red candle

- Ginger oil

- Rose quartz

Instructions:

Rub ginger oil into the red candle. Place the pink candles on the altar in a triangle, with one to the North, one to the East, and one to the West. Place the red candle in the center of the triangle. Light the pink candles, then hold the rose quartz in both hands with your eyes closed.

Visualize the feeling of being incredibly, unconditionally loved, allowing the feeling to grow as you strengthen your focus. When you're ready, open your eyes, and place the rose quartz just above the North pink candle. State your intention, and light the red candle, visualizing your personal power streaming through the flame and up into the Universe.

WATER SPELLS

Magical Water for Stress Relief

Crystal elixirs* have long been used in magical and healing traditions for a variety of purposes.

Try the simple transformative power of an amethyst elixir to clear away any energetic patterns resulting from built-up stress, resentment, or other negative states of mind. Amethyst calms nerves and strong emotions, relieves tension, and helps rebalance oversensitivity. First, cleanse and charge the amethyst with your specific intention. You can say, "*I clear away all stress/fear/anger regarding* _____."

Place it in a glass, pour in at least one cup of purified water, and cover. Leave the glass in moonlight or sunlight for at least 4 hours, or longer in cloudy conditions. When it's time to use your elixir, uncover it, state your intention again, and take seven sips. State the intention one more time, and drink most of the remaining water, leaving a little at the bottom of the glass. Dip your index finger into the glass, close your eyes, and trace a circle with the water on your forehead. Take a deep breath. Then, thank the water and the stone for their assistance.

*Before using any other crystal in an elixir, be sure to research it! Many crystals and stones are toxic to the body and should not be placed in drinking water.

Problem-Solving Sleep Spell

Tricky problems and difficult decisions are often a cause of poor sleep. This spell helps hand those worries over to the Universe while we get to the important business of quality rest! Very often, the needed solution or answer will arise the day after this spell is performed, though, depending on the circumstances, it may evolve more slowly.

You will need:

- Sleep-aiding tea, such as a blend of chamomile, spearmint, and lemongrass—make your own or use a nice commercial blend.

- 1 bowl—glass or ceramic, but not plastic

- 1 cup of water

- Dried lavender or lavender essential oil

- Moonstone or citrine

- 1 white tea light

Instructions:

Make and steep the tea as you do the following:

Hold the moonstone or citrine and focus on your question. (*Don't* focus on what you think may be the possible answers, or dwell on the apparent lack of solutions—simply focus on the question or problem itself.)

Place it in the bowl, and pour in the water. Light the tea light. Thank the Universe for all you will learn from the experience of the particular question/problem, as well as for its answer or solution. Sprinkle the lavender oil or herb into the water.

Drink the tea while meditating on something positive and unrelated to the problem or question. If the problem/question arises in your mind, keep letting it go, without judgement.

GOING FORWARD

These are just a few suggestions for consciously working with the Elements in your magic. As you develop your Craft, it's best to create your own spells and charms according to your intuition and connection with the Spirit of the Universe. Continue to read widely and always disregard information or suggestions that don't feel right to you. Most importantly, continue to cultivate your energetic relationship with the living world around us.

CONCLUSION

Many people first learn of the Wicca religion in the context of Magic and Witchcraft.

Although there is *far* more to Wicca than Witchcraft, I wanted to create a guide that helped newcomers and seasoned Witches alike to learn about the properties of the Elements that make up our Universe—as well as providing knowledge for readers who want to practice Witchcraft. After all, a great number of Wiccans *do* practice Witchcraft, whether on special occasions such as the Sabbats or as part of their daily routine, and as such, the information is important.

Of course, the way Magic and Witchcraft is portrayed in Hollywood is *very* different from how it is practiced in reality. However, the only thing that really matters is to always practice Witchcraft from a good place, and with good intent—you should never perform spellwork that deliberately seeks to harm another person, or encourages them to act against their will. Love spells are a great example of this, as, although love is a positive emotion, forcing a specific person to fall in love with you is highly manipulative.

This isn't an issue for most Wiccans—our appreciation of nature and the world around us means we are a peaceful bunch! However, for anyone planning on practicing Witchcraft for mischievous ends, the *Threefold Law* is highly ingrained into the Wiccan belief systems. This essentially says that whatever intent you send out into the Universe—in other words, good or bad—will come back to you three times as great. While some Wiccans will disagree over the existence of this cosmic 'law,' it is still a useful guideline to follow, and encourages all of us to be better human beings.

In this guide, I have attempted to take an unbiased approach wherever possible; however, as nothing with Wicca is set in stone, my own experiences as a practicing Wiccan may have influenced certain sections of the book. I have tried to be open and informative about the differing beliefs among Wiccans, and make reference to them where relevant, but some information presented will undoubtedly be influenced by my own journey and understanding of the topics.

To become a practicing Wiccan you do not have to share all of the beliefs I hold, or the ones presented in this guide. If something doesn't *feel* right to you, you're free to find your own path, and incorporate the beliefs and practices that *do* resonate with you. For many Wiccans, their beliefs are constantly changing with every new experience they face. My advice to you is to keep an open mind, as what you believe to be true today could alter a great deal tomorrow.

In my opinion, this is the best thing about Wicca: it is a lifelong journey, on which you will never stop learning!

I will leave you with that thought, though I sincerely hope that this guide to the Elements has given you a better understanding of the Universe and the world you inhabit. I have included a number of tables of correspondence at the end of this guide, which should prove useful as a reference point for any further study of the Elements.

I sincerely hope you enjoyed learning about Wicca and Witchcraft with me, and I would love for you to become a regular practitioner—by following the outlines in Part Three, you have everything you need to get started. However, if this is the end of your Wiccan journey, I hope you have learned something new, and that you better understand the belief system of the wonderful people who practice Wicca.

Thank you one more time for reading.

Blessed Be.

TABLES OF CORRESPONDENCE

These tables of correspondence illustrate various qualities and associations of tangible objects like crystals and stones, herbs, and oils, as well as intangible phenomena like colors, directions, and astrological signs.

Included here are tables of correspondence between the Elements and their various associations, including physical objects used to represent them in ritual and magic.

The information here is by no means complete, but is intended as a basic reference as you explore your practice of the Craft through an Elemental lens. Utilizing the tools and "ingredients" listed here can help you strengthen your connection with the Elements, and therefore with the powers of the Universe.

Try working with the stones, herbs, tools, etc. that you feel an affinity with, as well as introducing yourself to new ones from time to time.

TABLE ONE: ELEMENTS AND SPIRITUAL ASSOCIATIONS

Elements	Primary Qualities	Magical Purposes	Astrological Signs
Earth	Stability, discipline, prosperity, abundance	Employment, business, money, success in endeavors, fertility	Capricorn, Taurus, Virgo
Air	Intellect, communication, imagination, harmony	Creativity, concentration, inspiration, psychic abilities	Aquarius, Gemini, Libra
Fire	Passion, illumination, transformation, enthusiasm	Joy, love, strength, willpower, resolving anger	Aries, Leo, Sagittarius
Water	Emotion, sensitivity, intuition, empathy	Healing, purification, friendship issues, general well-being	Pisces, Cancer, Scorpio
Spirit	None	All	All

Elements	Cardinal Direction	Season	Animals
Earth	North	Winter	Wolf, bear, ant, bull and cow, horse, deer, dog
Air	East	Spring	Raven, hummingbird, most other birds and winged insects, spider
Fire	South	Summer	Fox, lion, tiger, lizard, praying mantis
Water	West	Autumn	Dolphin, turtle, swan, whale, most other sea animals and sea birds
Spirit	Center	All	All

TABLE TWO: ELEMENTS AND PHYSICAL ASSOCIATIONS

Elements	Ritual Tools	Colors	Crystals and Stones
Earth	Pentacle, bowl of salt or earth	Green	Jade, pyrite, moss agate, tourmaline
Air	Wand, incense, bell, feathers	Yellow	Aventurine, mottled jasper, turquoise, topaz
Fire	Candle, athame, incense	Red	Amber, bloodstone, garnet, tiger's eye
Water	Chalice	Blue	Amethyst, aquamarine, lapis lazuli, moonstone
Spirit	Magic circle, positive intention	Violet, white, black	Jet, onyx, quartz crystal

Elements	Herbs	Essential Oils
Earth	Horehound, moss, mugwort	Cypress, honeysuckle, oakmoss
Air	Red clover, comfrey leaf, dandelion	Frankincense, lemon balm, lavender
Fire	Basil, cayenne, nettles	Bergamot, ginger, rosemary
Water	Catnip, hibiscus flower, passion flower	Lemon, chamomile, sandalwood
Spirit	All, but especially mistletoe	All

SUGGESTIONS FOR FURTHER READING

Please note that this is a very brief list. Many other interesting and useful resources are available in print and online.

Ellen Dugan, *Natural Witchery: Intuitive, Personal & Practical Magick* (2007)

Peter Tompkins and Christopher Bird, *The Secret Life of Plants* (1973)

Masaro Emoto, *Messages From Water and the Universe* (2010)

Itzhak Bentov, *Stalking the Wild Pendulum: On the Mechanics of Consciousness* (1977)

John C. Briggs and F. David Peat, *Looking Glass Universe: The Emerging Science of Wholeness* (1986)

David Rankine and Sorita d'Este, *Practical Elemental Magick: Working the Magick of Air Fire Water & Earth in the Western Esoteric Tradition* (2008)

WICCA

MOON
MAGIC

*A Wiccan's Guide and Grimoire for
Working Magic with Lunar Energies*

LISA CHAMBERLAIN

CONTENTS

INTRODUCTION

If you're reading this book, you probably already know, or at least suspect, that the Moon is magic. You may have even sought it out now and then in the clear night sky and gazed upon its majestic radiance. Perhaps you've witnessed its quiet presence in the daytime sky as well.

Many people find themselves in thrall to the silvery, mysterious energy of the Moon no matter what their spiritual or magical leanings. But for those who practice Wicca and other forms of Paganism, the Moon is a vital presence with much to teach us—about the natural rhythms of the Universe, the eternal powers of Nature, and the magical potential that is ours to tap into when we align our intentions with lunar energy.

Of course, modern practitioners of Witchcraft and magic are hardly the only people with the knowledge that the Moon is more than a giant space rock orbiting the Earth. Since the first stirrings of human civilization, the Moon has played an important role in the myths and practices of cultures around the world.

It was valued for millennia as a source of light and a way of measuring time, and like its counterpart, the Sun, it has been linked with many gods and goddesses. In both myth and magic, the Moon has been universally associated with many central concerns of human existence: love, passion, fertility, mystery, death and rebirth, and the afterlife, just to name a few.

Its magical significance was understood throughout Western Europe before the widespread domination of Christianity all but eradicated the indigenous religions of the region. Thankfully, over the last century or so, that ancient knowledge has been brought back out of the shadows, and as Wicca and other modern Pagan traditions continue to evolve and spread, more and more people are now able to take advantage of the Moon's transformational power.

This book is for anyone wanting to learn more about the connections between the Moon and the practice of magic, regardless of religious or spiritual orientation. While much of the information comes from a Wiccan perspective, and it is written to include newcomers to Wicca, the guide is not primarily focused on the Wiccan religion.

Aside from a basic overview of the Moon's role in Wiccan practice, the larger focus is on understanding the power of the Moon and its implications for an approach to magic that is aligned with lunar cycles. The practical elements are largely accessible enough for beginners, but those with more magical experience are still likely to find plenty of new ideas, concepts, and tips to enhance their practice.

So whether you follow a particular tradition of Wicca, Witchcraft, or another Pagan path, or an eclectic combination of all three—or even if you're simply just curious!—you are bound to find useful material within these pages. After all, the Moon belongs to no single religion or spiritual practice, and your connection with the Moon, and with magic itself, is uniquely your own.

In Part One, we'll examine some of the existing knowledge of the Moon in the wider "mainstream" world, including our modern scientific understanding of its relationship to the Earth as well as social and cultural observations of its effects on human beings and other animals all over the planet.

Then, we'll introduce the Wiccan perspective on the Moon, specifically in terms of the beliefs and practices surrounding this very important celestial body— the Moon's identification with the Triple Goddess, the celebration of Esbats, and the sacred act of drawing down the Moon are touched on here.

We'll also take a brief look at a related Pagan tradition of observing astrological factors that influence the Moon's energy. This initial tour sets us up for Part Two, where we'll dive into an expansive discussion of the lunar cycle.

Not many people who are new to magic have been in the habit of paying daily attention to the rhythms of the Moon's orbit around the

Earth. In Part Two of this guide, we'll outline the lunar cycle in detail, charting its appearance in the sky as it moves through each phase, and explaining the key terminology used to track the Moon's progressions from one phase to the next.

We'll then lay out some systems of correspondences, used by many Witches, that align the lunar cycle with seasonal processes in Nature. These correspondences can help you gain a more intuitive sense of the Moon's energy at any particular point in the cycle, and harness that energy more effectively in your magical work. We'll also take a look at two special occasions that are optimal for lunar magic—Blue Moons and Lunar Eclipses—before moving on to the practical magic featured in Part Three.

The spells, recipes, and other hands-on information in the third and final section of this guide are all specifically related to the Moon. You'll find spellwork for each major lunar phase—New, waxing, Full, and waning—as well as workings for a Blue Moon and a Lunar Eclipse. You'll also find Tables of Correspondence for Moon-associated magical ingredients to help you create your own unique spells and rituals.

However, this lunar "Book of Shadows"—or grimoire—is just the beginning when it comes to living more magically in tune with the Moon. To that end, we also include a suggested reading list at the end of the guide, for those who wish to further pursue this fascinating aspect of Witchcraft and magic.

So enjoy your journey through these lunar pages. Once you've read this book you'll never look at the Moon the same way again!

Blessed Be.

PART ONE

THE MAGICAL MOON

NIGHT GUIDE
OF THE ANCIENTS

If you live in a city, surrounded by artificial light from street lamps, buildings, and automobiles, it's very possible to live your entire existence without ever truly noticing the Moon. You may occasionally glimpse it in the night sky, but the light from the Moon will almost never be distinguishable from any other source of light.

If you live in a rural area, on the other hand, you have most likely reveled in the way the Full Moon can seem to light up everything in your environment, and you are probably more accustomed to noticing the Moon on a fairly regular basis.

But whether or not you're in the habit of observing the Moon, you and everyone else on the planet are affected, however subtly, by this mysterious satellite orbiting the Earth.

Of course, in the centuries before the advent of modern technology, everyone was definitely paying attention to the Moon. Not only was moonlight the only source of nighttime illumination other than fire, but the regular phases of the Moon's ever-shifting appearance in the sky were used to mark time.

In fact, to this day many cultures continue to follow a lunar calendar, often using it concurrently with the solar (or "Gregorian") calendar used throughout most of the world. (This is why the holidays celebrated by Jewish, Muslim, and Chinese people are on different dates each year. Even the date for the Christian holiday of Easter is determined by the Moon, falling on the Sunday following the first Full Moon after the Spring Equinox.)

It was certainly not lost on those who lived near the oceans that the Moon has an effect on the tides, and hunters all over the planet would have noted the behavioral patterns of animals based on the cycles of the Moon, and planned their hunting and fishing activities accordingly. The Moon was taken into account by agrarian cultures as well, governing the best times for planting and harvesting crops. Indeed, the Moon's importance to the survival of our ancestors was ultimately just as significant as that of the Sun.

Given the impact that this celestial body had on the daily lives of humans in ancient times, it's no surprise that the Moon figured prominently in religious practices around the globe. Indeed, Moon worship is found in the oldest religious writings of ancient Egypt, Babylonia, China and India, and deities from a wide variety of ancient cultures are associated with the Moon.

In some traditions, the Moon's ever-repeating pattern of disappearing and reappearing was associated with concepts of life, death, and rebirth. Many agricultural societies held the Moon to be a female ruler of vegetation cycles. The concept of "yin" and "yang" energies in ancient Chinese philosophy ascribed the Moon to yin, or female energy, balancing out the yang energy of the Sun.

These and other spiritual traditions from the pre-Christian world have influenced many of the beliefs and practices found within Wicca and other contemporary Pagan religions. The incorporation of lunar energies into magical work is also inspired by ancient beliefs.

But before we delve into the ways in which today's Wiccans and other Witches work with the Moon, let's take a brief look at some of what we've learned since the ancient days about this enigmatic giant rock slowly whirling around our planet.

THE 21ST-CENTURY MOON

Over the last several decades, our human relationship to the Moon has reached a whole new level, as astronauts have actually journeyed there and scientists have been learning much about the cosmos from their findings ever since.

And while we don't need a scientific understanding of the Moon to appreciate its spiritual significance to humanity or its effect on our individual lives, it's worthwhile to take a look at our celestial friend from the perspective of those who have studied it most closely.

ORIGINS AND ORBIT

The most widely accepted theory of the Moon's origins involves a collision between Earth and a giant asteroid roughly the size of Mars, which happened 4.5 billion years ago. The astral debris resulting from the crash was caught in Earth's gravitational pull, orbiting around the globe until it ultimately coalesced to form the Moon.

Another theory states that the Moon was actually a chunk of the Earth that was somehow torn from its crust and mantle and flung out into orbit.

Either scenario can help to explain why the Earth and the Moon have plenty in common beneath the surface. Although the crust of the Earth is made of rather different mineral material than the crust of the

Moon, scientists have found that beneath the Earth's crust are several of the minerals that make up the bulk of the Moon's composition.

So it would seem that one way or another, the Moon and the Earth have a special connection, which you might say is symbolized by the gravitational pull that Earth has on the Moon, and the reciprocal pull that the Moon has on Earth's oceans.

The Moon's orbit around the Earth takes approximately 28 days, which is the length of a lunar month. During this orbit, the Moon's changing position relative to the Earth and the Sun causes different amounts of its surface to be illuminated, resulting in the four "phases" we identify from our perspective on Earth: **new**, **waxing**, **full**, and **waning**.

The **New Moon** occurs when the Moon is between the Earth and the Sun, so that the Sun's illumination of the Moon cannot be seen. As the Moon's movement continues, more and more of the Moon is illuminated—this is the **waxing phase**.

Once the Earth is between the Moon and the Sun, we can see a total illumination at the **Full Moon**. This illumination is then reduced again during the **waning phase**, until we once again cannot see the Moon at all.

As for the tidal effect, this is the Moon's gravity tugging on the Earth itself. The oceans on the side of Earth nearest the Moon are rising toward the Moon, while the vast waters on the other side of the globe are bulging due to the Earth's being pulled toward the Moon as well. Because the Earth is also rotating on its own axis, this high tide occurs twice a day, as does the low tide on the other end of the ever-shifting ocean.

THE BODY AND THE PSYCHE

Scientists have also observed some effects of the Moon's cycles on the behavior of animals, particularly when it comes to mating and hunting. These patterns occur both in nocturnal animals and animals primarily active during the day, and even show up in certain insects.

Furthermore, several species of birds have been seen to change their communication patterns around the Full Moon. Ocean life is also affected in the sense that high and low tides shape sea animals' behavior. Even household pets appear to be affected by the Moon, as it has been shown that cats and dogs end up in veterinary emergency rooms from accidents occurring on nights when there's a waxing or Full Moon!

Of course, humans are animals too, and as such are no less susceptible to the effects of the Moon's perpetual transformations.

It has been noted since ancient times that women's menstrual cycles tend to be in rhythm with the Moon. Ovulation and conception rates are lower at the New Moon, and tend to peak around the days leading up to, and the day of, the Full Moon. Furthermore, at least one study has shown that more births occur during times when the Moon is closest to the Earth, meaning that its gravitational pull is at its strongest.

The Moon has also been shown to affect sleep patterns, and even the outcomes of surgery—apparently, people undergoing emergency heart surgery fare better during the days around the Full Moon than during other places in the Moon's cycle.

Interestingly, what science has not been able to "prove," so far, is a phenomenon that is well-known to many who work in various human service occupations: people just seem to get a little "loony" during the Full Moon.

While no studies have confirmed that this is true, you can ask just about any bartender, child care worker, or emergency room attendant and you'll hear tales of increased accidents, erratic behavior, and downright "moodiness" during these times. In fact, the word "lunatic," rooted in the Latin word for "moon" (*luna*) comes from the belief that the changes in the Moon's appearance could cause periodic insanity.

But perhaps the biggest indicator of our awareness that the Full Moon can have a dramatic influence on humans is the archetype of the werewolf, doomed to transform from man to vicious dog every 28 days.

Generally speaking, the werewolf serves as an exaggerated and extreme symbol of the Moon's power. All the same, if you're interested enough in the Moon to be reading this book, it's highly likely you've already noticed that both the Full and the New Moon can be times of heightened sensitivity, restlessness, anxiety and/or a lack of energy, depending on how the Moon affects you personally.

For example, some people find that thinking clearly is more of a challenge around the New Moon, while others experience extreme sleepiness. It's not uncommon to feel a sense of "extra gravity" around both New and Full Moons, and intuitive types often enjoy an enhanced connection to the psychic energies swirling around in the atmosphere.

Indeed, despite how much we may have learned about the Moon on a "factual" level in the recent past, this celestial partner of the Earth still retains some very magical mysteries. This is well understood by Wiccans and other Witches, for whom the Moon is a central, sacred part of spiritual and magical practice.

We'll take a look now at some core elements of the Wiccan religion as they relate to the Moon, as well as a few other associated traditions followed by many Wiccans, Witches, and others in the contemporary Pagan world.

THE WICCAN MOON

First and foremost, the Moon is the ultimate symbol of the Goddess, the all-encompassing divine feminine in the Wiccan cosmology.

Consort to the God, whose projective, masculine energy is represented by the Sun, the Goddess embodies the receptive, feminine energy that nourishes all life. She is the night to the God's day, the Water to the God's Fire, the yin to the God's yang.

As the Moon, she appeals to the mysterious, psychic, and magical qualities within our human selves. Many Wiccans so strongly identify the Moon with the Goddess that they speak of the Moon with feminine pronouns ("she," "her") rather than the genderless "it." But regardless of the pronouns used by worshippers of the Goddess, the essence of the Moon's magical energy is always female.

Those who worship the Goddess under a specific name often identify her with a moon-associated goddess from an ancient pantheon, such as the Roman Diana, the Greek Selene, or the Celtic Rhiannon.

Others may worship her as the Egyptian Isis or Bast, even though these did not originate as Moon goddesses. Actually, the ancient Egyptians first associated the Moon with masculine deities, while the Sun's deities were often feminine. It wasn't until the cultures of ancient Egypt and Greece intermingled that Egyptian goddesses became associated with the Moon.

The Celts were also diverse about gender when it came to deities. Both the goddess Brighid and the god Lugh have solar associations, while the lunar deities include the god Oisin as well as several goddesses.

When it comes to the Moon in contemporary Wicca, however, the divine is always feminine.

THE TRIPLE GODDESS

It should be noted that in most Wiccan traditions, the Earth is also viewed as a representation of the Goddess.

Given the co-creative relationship between the Earth and the Moon, there is no inherent contradiction in this overlap—both are essential to sustaining life. However, where the Earth is typically seen as a "Mother Goddess," the Goddess of the Moon actually has three different identities, or aspects: the **Maiden**, the **Mother**, and the **Crone**.

This expanded form is the **Triple Moon Goddess**: the multifaceted deity whose diversity of roles both mirrors the cycles of the Moon— waxing, Full, and waning, and personifies the three phases of the lives of women—before, during, and after the childbearing years.

And although women experience these events in a linear sequence, their lives are also part of a cycle, because Wiccans believe in reincarnation. After the death of the Crone comes rebirth, and the new journey leading back to the realm of the Maiden.

While the concepts surrounding the Triple Moon Goddess (also known simply as the **Triple Goddess**) largely originate with the work of spiritualists in the mid-1900s, there is precedent for a three-fold feminine deity in ancient written and pictorial artifacts.

Among Wiccans, two well-known goddesses with triple associations are the Celtic Brighid, goddess of healing, poetry, and smithcraft; and the Greek Hera, who appears in some myths in three different roles: Girl, Woman, and Widow. Neither was particularly associated with the Moon in ancient times, but there are some links between three separate Moon goddesses who form a kind of trinity, such as Artemis, Selene and Hecate.

Many Wiccans worship the Triple Moon Goddess in a similar fashion, whether they are all from the same ancient pantheon or "borrowed" from different cultural groups. For example, she may be Rhiannon in the Maiden aspect, the Greek Demeter as the Mother, and Hecate as the Crone. These designations are based on the characteristics of the goddesses and their roles as they appear in their native mythologies, and are not generally interchangeable.

Furthermore, each goddess has her own magical domains, also rooted in original mythology, and so can be called upon for assistance with related magical goals. These correspondences are linked to both her identity and her archetypal role.

If you're interested in learning more about working magic with any aspect of the Triple Goddess, it's worth reading the rich mythology surrounding these ancient deities and exploring connections with any you feel intuitively drawn to.

Like the individual goddesses who represent them, each aspect of the Triple Goddess has her own archetypal identity. Each symbolizes various elements in Nature, including animal and plant life, seasons and times of day, and different characteristics of the human experience.

Although the emphasis is on the feminine, each of the associations within the domain of the Triple Goddess is relevant to both males and females, since all of us contain both masculine and feminine energies within our psyches.

Likewise, we all experience our own cycles of birth, maturation and death over the course of our lives, whether it be in regard to our relationships, projects, ambitions, etc. In one way or another, we all resonate with all three aspects of the Triple Goddess at various points in our personal journeys.

Let's briefly meet the Maiden, Mother, and Crone as they exist in the Wiccan cosmology. Then in Part Two, we'll take a closer look at the phases of the Moon they represent, including the many different possibilities for magic that are supported by these lunar rhythms.

THE MAIDEN

The Maiden aspect of the Triple Goddess emerges with the crescent Moon, and reigns during the waxing days as the Moon grows toward Full.

She represents the youth and innocence of life before motherhood, and so is associated with all things "new": the dawn, the sunrise, the Spring, young animals, and all that is ripening into fullness.

The Maiden assists with activities involving creativity, beauty, exploration, self-discovery and self-expression.

She supports the characteristics of self-confidence, intelligence and independence.

Goddesses who typically represent the Maiden include the Greek goddesses Persephone and Artemis, the Celtic Rhiannon, and the Nordic Freya, and many others from around the globe.

THE MOTHER

The Mother Goddess is aligned with the days just before, during and after the Full Moon.

Having matured from Maiden to Mother, her time is the afternoon, when the day's light is at its strongest, and her season is the lush full swing of Summer.

As the one who brings forth new life, she is the goddess most associated with manifestation of all kinds, as well as adulthood, responsibility, and tending and nurturing what has come into being.

As the symbol of the Full Moon, she is often revered as the most powerful of the three aspects of the Triple Goddess.

The Mother is often worshipped in the guise of the Roman Ceres, the Greek Demeter and Selene, and the Celtic Badb and Danu, among others.

THE CRONE

As the Moon wanes, becoming less and less visible with each passing day, the Crone steps into her power.

The most mysterious of the three aspects, she is associated with sunset and night, and Autumn and Winter—the darkest times in the cycle of life and death on Earth.

Finished now with the duties of motherhood, the Goddess turns her focus to the domains of death and ultimate rebirth. Her understanding of these cycles makes her the wise elder, and she supports experiences involving aging, completions, prophecies and visions, transformation, and death—both literal and figurative.

The Crone reigns during the dark of the Moon, patiently tending the nights until the New Moon returns.

She is represented by a wide cultural range of goddesses, including the Russian Baba Yaga, the Greek Hecate, and the Celtic Morrigan and Cailleach Bear.

THE ESBATS

While every aspect of the Triple Goddess—and corresponding Moon phase—is sacred to Wiccans, the divine feminine is particularly honored at every Full Moon.

These celebrations are called **Esbats**, and occur either 12 or 13 times per calendar year, depending on how the lunar calendar lines up with the solar (or "Gregorian") calendar. While the God is honored at the Sabbats—the four solar holidays and four cross-quarter days that make up the Wheel of the Year—the Esbats belong to the Goddess.

Some Wiccans call the Esbats the "second Wheel of the Year," but this doesn't mean that Full Moon celebrations are less important than the Sabbats. Wicca is rooted in gender polarity—the Universe being made up of both male and female energies in equal parts—and so the lunar/Esbat cycle is every bit as central as the solar/Sabbat cycle.

The details and particular focus of the Esbat rituals vary widely among covens and solitary Wiccans. Very often, the focus of the rituals will align with the time of year, and/or honoring a specific aspect of the Goddess. For example, an Esbat taking place in late Autumn may be devoted to a Crone goddess such as Kali (Hindu) or Badb (Celtic), while a Spring Esbat might focus on Maiden goddesses like Diana (Greek) or Ostara (Saxon).

Many covens and informal circles will work magic together, since the Moon's power is particularly strong on these occasions. Magical goals include individual intentions as well as communal and even global needs, such as healing, abundance, and respect for the Earth and her natural resources.

Just as each solar Sabbat celebrates a distinct point along the Wheel—such as the height of Summer at Litha/Solstice or the beginning of the harvest season at Lammas/Lughnasa—each Full Moon has its own distinct energy. For example, the Full Moons of late Summer and Autumn tend to have a more electric feeling than the quiet, more subtle energies of Winter Moons.

Each Full Moon also has its own name, which generally honors an aspect of the natural world, agricultural cycles, animal behavior, and even human activities. There are several names for each Moon, which are borrowed from various Native American traditions, as well as the ancient Celts and, more rarely, Chinese traditions. For example, the Full Moon in January may be known as the Ice Moon, the Wolf Moon, or the Stay Home Moon.

The most commonly used names in Wiccan traditions are the following:

Month	Moon Name
January	Cold Moon (also Hunger)
February	Quickening Moon (also Snow)
March	Storm Moon (also Sap)
April	Wind Moon (also Pink)
May	Flower Moon (also Milk)
June	Sun Moon (also Strong Sun and Rose)

Month	Moon Name
July	Blessing Moon (also Thunder)
August	Corn Moon (also Grain)
September	Harvest Moon
October	Blood Moon
November	Mourning Moon (also Frost)
December	Long Nights Moon

It's important to note that not every coven meets at the Full Moon to hold their Esbats. Some choose to celebrate at the New Moon instead, while others will strive to observe both points on the "second Wheel."

Solitary Witches often observe both New and Full Moons as well, and may also honor the Half Moons with at least a small ritual or candle-lighting.

In the general sense of the word, "Esbat" really refers to any ritual that honors the Moon and the Goddess.

DRAWING DOWN THE MOON

One very highly significant ritual that takes place at every Full Moon Esbat is the act of drawing down the Moon. This is a transformative process that brings the energy of the Moon—and therefore, the energy of the Goddess—into the physical body of the Witch.

In a coven ceremony, the High Priestess will perform the act, usually with words of invocation, and become the human embodiment of the Goddess on behalf of the group. Depending on the tradition followed by the coven, this can be an elaborate ritual with many spoken elements, gestures, and the use of symbolic ritual tools, or it may be fairly simple, yet elegant.

The same is true for solitary Wiccans who make drawing down the Moon part of their practice—while many follow older, more established traditions, many more approach drawing down the Moon in a more individualized manner. They may use the athame, or ritual knife, to symbolically draw the Moon's power into their bodies, or they may simply stand silently under the Moon with their palms turned upward.

This sacred ritual creates a powerful experience for the participant, who may feel strong physical or emotional sensations after connecting with the Goddess in this way, and it's a unique experience for every individual.

Ideally, drawing down the Moon takes place at the exact moment that the Moon becomes Full. If this isn't possible, Wiccans will try to hold the ritual as closely as possible to that moment, which is typically the night before.

Standing outside directly under the Moon is considered to be the most powerful location for this work, but standing indoors at a window and/or with a candle dedicated to the Goddess is also effective.

Strictly speaking, drawing down the Moon is a Full Moon ritual, but some eclectic Wiccans incorporate it into their practice at other times during the lunar cycle as well. In every instance, the energy harnessed from this connection with the Goddess is used to charge the ensuing ritual activities, including any magical work undertaken at this time.

THE WITCH, THE MOON, AND THE STARS

While the specific practices described above originate with traditional Wicca, working with the feminine power of the Moon is not exclusive to this spiritual path.

Many who identify as Witches but not Wiccans, and plenty of those who identify with the more general term Pagan, also honor and connect with the Moon at various times throughout the lunar cycle. Their ways of doing so are quite diverse, and many eclectic types create their own rituals and practices, rather than following established traditions.

For example, a Witch whose practice is steeped in herbal knowledge and gardening might choose to plant seeds at the New Moon in order to honor the new life that this phase represents. In lieu of a formal ritual, a group of like-minded Witches and other Pagans might simply hold a potluck feast at the Full Moon. Non-Wiccans may or may not worship the divine feminine in the form of a deity, though many do revere the Goddess and/or ancient goddesses associated with the Moon.

Furthermore, many Wiccans and non-Wiccans alike take astrological circumstances into account when working with the Full Moon, in addition to (or instead of) focusing on seasonal influences or aspects of the Goddess. Some traditions identify the current Sun sign and name the Moon accordingly, rather than using one of the more traditional names explained above. The ritual and magic surrounding this Full Moon are centered on the attributes of the Zodiac sign.

For example, the Full Moon that occurs between October 23 and November 21 is called the Scorpio Moon. This is a time to reflect on the nature of illusion and to engage in piercing through illusions that are blocking our progress in some way. Magic at this time may be worked for protection from negativity, enhanced intuition, or deeper connection with one's inner power.

Alternatively, some Witches work according to the sign the Moon is in, so that the Full Moon occurring between the dates given above would be called the Taurus Moon. The Moon is always in the opposite sign from the Sun when it's Full, so this is fairly easy to pinpoint once you're familiar with the Zodiac wheel.

Given this lunar relationship between the opposite signs, some traditions actually incorporate both signs (e.g. Scorpio and Taurus) into their Full Moon rituals, for a balanced approach to tuning into the energies of this powerful phase in the cycle.

Astrological considerations don't only apply to the Full Moon, however. The Moon spends approximately two and a half days in each sign during its orbit around the Earth, and those who are attuned to these subtle shifts will notice certain patterns in circumstances and behavior that correspond to each sign.

For example, when the Moon is in Aries, people tend to feel more assertive and even argumentative, and events may unfold rapidly and then come to an equally quick end.

Astrological information can be used to guide magical work as well. In the case of Aries, which is located at the beginning of the Zodiac, spells involving beginnings are favored.

When the Moon is en route from one sign to the next, it is considered to be "void of course." Many Wiccans and other Witches recommend abstaining from spellwork at this time, as the lunar energies are "on break," so to speak, and magic is likely to have little effect. These "void" periods are just a few hours long on average, but occasionally last for a day or more.

Those who are really into astrology might also take into account the Moon's position in relation to the planets, particularly when an alignment with one or more planets has a significant energetic effect on events, emotions, and other circumstances. However, this is more advanced knowledge than most people find necessary, at least when it comes to ritual and magic.

Too much detail can definitely end up distracting one's focus in this regard. There's really no need to become an astrology buff in order to work with the Moon's magical energy. If you feel called to learn more and incorporate the planets and the stars into your relationship with the Moon, go for it. If not, that's perfectly fine, too.

DIVING DEEPER

Since the beginning of human history, the Moon has figured into our daily lives in one way or another, even if most people living in today's Western mainstream culture no longer realize it. Various cultures around the world continue to recognize, appreciate, and celebrate the Moon's power, with a wide range of traditions and practices for harnessing this special energy for magic.

Here, we have briefly examined the main elements of the Moon's role in the core beliefs and practices of Wicca, as well as a few related practices that incorporate older astrological traditions. Next, we'll take a closer look at the mysterious power of lunar energy and a much more comprehensive view of the lunar cycle.

You'll find a detailed breakdown of each phase of the cycle, including the ever-changing appearance of the Moon in the sky as it orbits the Earth and the magical associations of each phase. From New to Full, to Dark and back to New again, the never-ending cycle of the Moon presents a rich variety of opportunities to tune into the energies of the natural world and enhance your spellwork.

Indeed, the potential for Moon magic goes far beyond working spells under the Full Moon, as we will see in the discussion of each lunar phase. We'll look at relationships between the lunar cycle and the Wheel of the Year, as well as growth cycles as observed in wild and cultivated plant life.

These correspondences can help you deepen your magical practice on a profound level as you tune in to the connections between your own life and the ever-shifting tides of waxing and waning, attracting and releasing, growing and dying back. Adopting a practice of living in rhythm with the Moon can open up amazing pathways to a deeper connection with the Universe, and enhance your quality of life.

Finally, there are two aspects of the Moon's relationship with magic that have not been discussed in this initial overview: Blue Moons and Lunar Eclipses. These special events are observed and honored by Wiccans, Witches, and other Pagans, and are often even noted in the mainstream world.

The rare energy of Blue Moons and the highly charged energy of Eclipses can enhance magic like no other force on Earth or in the cosmos, and the opportunities they present should not be missed. However, it's more useful to examine these phenomena once the lunar cycle is more fully understood.

So let's dive deeper now into the magical waters of the Moon.

PART TWO

RHYTHMS OF THE MOON

LUNAR ENERGY AND MAGIC

Have you ever heard the saying, "it must be the Moon?"

Usually used in a joking manner to explain away any strange events or bizarre behavior witnessed when the Moon is Full, this phrase has much more truth to it than most people would believe.

Mainstream culture tends to laugh off the notion of Moon-influenced feelings and behavior, but, as we saw in Part One, the Moon does have effects on people and animals. This tends to be most obvious during the days surrounding the Full Moon, whether we're noticing unusual behavior in our pets or children, or feeling ourselves to be abnormally "moody."

But while you may already be aware that the "Full Moon effect" is not a myth, you may not realize that *all* phases of the Moon's cycle influence us on some level, however subtle it may be for those who aren't yet attuned to lunar energy.

Just as the Earth has its own energy, which is independent from the energy it receives from the Sun, the Moon, too, emits an energy that is subtle, yet distinctive. Unlike the Sun's masculine, projective energy, lunar energy is feminine and receptive. This is the energy of the Goddess.

This power has often been described as magnetic, which makes sense to anyone who has literally felt "pulled" in some way by the Moon. Some particularly sensitive people actually feel a physical tug in their bodies at the Full or New Moon, while others just notice a heightened sense of awareness to everything in their environment.

The way you personally respond to the Moon's energy will depend on many factors, including diet and exercise patterns, as well as influences in your astrological birth chart. Indeed, everyone's relationship with the Moon's cycle is unique, but if you start paying close attention to how you think and feel during each phase, you'll be better able to understand how these rhythms affect your personal power. Then you can use these discoveries to strengthen your magical abilities.

What does the Moon's energy have to do with magic? As multi-sensory beings, we are constantly interacting with unseen energies coming from every direction—from other people, from media, from the food we eat and the buildings we spend our days and nights in. Everything we interact with has an effect on our personal energetic makeup.

We tend to focus on what we experience through our five physical senses—sight, sound, touch, taste, and smell. But our sixth sense—intuition—is the most crucial mode of perception when it comes to magic. And the energy of the Moon is tailor-made for interacting with the energy of our intuition, which is also feminine, receptive, and magnetic in nature.

So when we consciously connect with lunar energy, we are opening up our own capacity to channel that energy into drawing what we desire to us, and releasing what we don't want from our lives. And when we do so in conscious harmony with the energetic rhythms of the Moon's cycle, we can truly amplify the power of our magical work.

TRACKING THE MOON

Before considering the relationship between the Moon and magic, however, it's important to identify the phases of the lunar cycle in more detail. After all, you can't truly take advantage of the opportunities that lunar energies present if you don't know what's happening in the sky when you're casting your spells!

Let's take a look now at two different frameworks for describing and tracking the movement of the Moon as it orbits the Earth, and then we'll discuss the magical opportunities that each phase presents.

LIGHT AND SHADOW

In the first framework, the Moon's cycle is tracked by its appearance in the sky.

It begins as a barely-detectable sliver at the New Moon. Over the next few days, the sliver becomes larger and more defined, almost resembling the tip of a fingernail—this is called the Crescent Moon. From here, the Moon continues to grow—or "wax"— on its way to becoming Full. At the mid-point between New and Full, we see the waxing Half Moon, with the illuminated half on the right and the shadowed half on the left.

As the circle begins to be filled out with light, it becomes "gibbous," a word used in astronomy to describe the bulging appearance of the Moon during the days just before and after it's completely Full. Finally, when the circle is completely lit, we are looking at the Full Moon.

In the days just after the Full point, the Moon is gibbous again, then continues to shrink—or "wane"—further back to Half. This time, the light half is on the left, with the shadowed half on the right.

More and more of the Moon is covered in shadow as it wanes back to its Crescent point, and then completely disappears. This window of time before it is visible again is the Dark Moon. Once the sliver returns, the cycle begins again.

MEASURING TIME

The other way of tracking the Moon's cycle is to divide it into four quarters, spread out over roughly 28 days. Each quarter lasts approximately seven days, adding up to create what we call the lunar "month."

The first quarter begins at the New Moon and ends at the waxing Half. The second quarter runs from there until the Full Moon. The third quarter begins immediately after the Moon turns Full and lasts until the waning Half Moon, and the fourth quarter closes out the cycle through the Dark Moon, ending just as the Moon reemerges into New.

It's interesting to note that while the two systems are not technically in conflict with each other, in terms of covering the full lunar cycle, there is something of an asymmetrical "glitch" when you try to align them. The ordered, even-numbered quarter system contains 4 units, which doesn't quite align with the 5 major marking points—New, Half, Full, Half, Dark—of the older, somewhat looser framework.

This is because the quarter system doesn't actually take the Dark Moon period into account. In reality, the Moon takes 29.5 days to complete its orbit, which is a number that 4 doesn't divide into equally, so there's a slight "lag" during the Dark time between the fourth and first quarters.

Furthermore, the period of amplified energetic influence that the Full Moon exerts is much longer than the brief period of time when it's fully illuminated. In the Witching world, the Full moon phase is actually considered to be 5 days long—from the two days before Full, when the Moon is still gibbous, until two days after, when the waning is just becoming visible.

Some people go even further, designating a full week to the Full Moon. But for the purposes of working with lunar energies, it can be argued that the Full Moon phase begins and ends when you *feel* it beginning and ending. To some extent, the entire lunar cycle is a bit like that. Remember, it's ultimately about your personal intuitive perception—your sixth sense.

Nonetheless, the quarter system may be more appealing to some, as it can be easier to keep track of. In fact, many calendars note the beginning mark of each quarter. And it's particularly helpful when you don't have the opportunity to go looking at the Moon every single night. (In fact, depending on where it is in its orbit and your own sleep schedule, you may not be able to see it at night.)

The truth is, it really doesn't matter how you track the phases, as long as you're at least aware of when the New and Full Moons occur—these are, after all, the two most energetically powerful times of the cycle.

So if you're new to paying close attention to the Moon, start by paying attention to these two points. As you get into the habit of "tracking the Moon" in this way, you'll find yourself attuning to the more subtle, continuous rhythms of the various energies of the Moon's complete cycle. You'll also get a better feel for timing your magic to align as closely as possible with each lunar phase.

Now that the full cycle has been more specifically illuminated, let's delve into the magical implications for working in harmony with the rhythms of the Moon.

MAGICAL TIMING AND THE LUNAR CYCLE

Generally speaking, the relationship between magic and the Moon can be summed up as follows: as the Moon grows, we work magic for increase; as it wanes, we work magic for decrease.

Another way to say it is that when you're seeking to bring something into your life, you work with the waxing Moon, and when you want to banish or release some unwanted element of your life, you work during the waning phase.

The transitional point between these two opposites is the Full Moon, a time of "harvest" as we celebrate what we have manifested over the first half of the cycle. We then essentially "clean up" afterward, identifying and releasing what is no longer needed throughout the second half of the cycle. At the New Moon, we set new intentions for the next cycle of manifestation, and on and on it goes.

The rhythm of this cycle can be visualized as the rhythm of the tides, which the Moon, of course, is causing. The waves grow bigger and come closer, covering more of the shoreline as the tide rises. The incoming surf peaks at high tide, and then recedes, exposing more and more shoreline until it reaches the low tide mark, and begins to rise again.

This is the basic framework, and yet there's much more to it than the simple dichotomy of "wax/wane," "flow, ebb," or "increase/decrease." Many Witches deepen their practice of working with the Moon by incorporating more complex systems of alignments and associations within the lunar cycle.

For starters, as we saw in Part One, those who worship the Triple Goddess will generally call upon the appropriate aspect when working magic aligned with the Moon—the Maiden is asked for assistance in the waxing phase, the Mother at the Full Moon, and the Crone when the Moon is on the wane.

Others may observe additional correspondences between the phases of the lunar cycle and the seasons, the Sabbats on the Wheel of the Year, and/or the growing cycles of plant life, which is the basis for so much of the symbolism inherent to Wicca and other forms of the Craft.

These systems can provide beautiful ways of further attuning to the Moon's subtle rhythms, as we will see next.

SEASONS AND SABBATS

Although it's the Earth's orbit around the Sun that is responsible for the turning of the seasons, the ever-shifting appearance of the Moon in the sky can be seen as a mirroring of the same cycle.

For example, Spring is the time of new life and increasing growth, which corresponds to the Moon's waxing phase. The Full Moon represents Summer, with its explosion of vegetation and the flourishing of young animal life, while the Autumn corresponds with the waning phase, as plants die back and animals prepare for the end of the warmer seasons. The Winter, then, is represented by the Dark Moon, as all life waits for the cycle to begin again.

This system of seasonal alignments can enhance our understanding of the subtle distinctions between the various magical aims that are most appropriate at different points in the lunar cycle.

However, it's rather unevenly distributed in terms of the actual length of seasons—after all, Summer and Winter are just as long as Spring and Autumn, so in a sense it's disproportionate to grant them only a few days of the Moon's cycle while the other seasons get nearly two weeks.

But if you're willing to expand the framework and go deeper into the Wheel of the Year, you'll find that there's a much more evenly-spaced system that truly illuminates the alignment between the patterns of the Sun and the Moon.

Using the eight Sabbats as a "map" of the Moon's travels, we can view the incremental shifts of the waxing and waning phases more closely, allowing for the "in-between" seasons to guide us into even more optimal timing of our magical efforts.

One way to do this is to match the Moon's quarter marks with the solar Sabbats. For example, the Full Moon can be represented by the Summer Solstice (also known in Wicca as Litha) and the New Moon by the Winter Solstice (or, Yule).

This would place each Half Moon at an equinox point—the waxing Half at Spring (Ostara) and the waning Half at Autumn (Mabon)—with the crescent and gibbous phases represented by the four Earth Sabbats: Imbolc, Beltane, Lughnasa and Samhain.

Then the days between Samhain and Yule, when the nights are the longest that they'll be all year, belong to the Dark Moon.

(Of course, if you live in the Southern Hemisphere, these correspondences run in reverse—or counter-clockwise—with Yule being the Summer Solstice and therefore the time of the Full Moon, and the New Moon aligning with Litha, and so on.)

This system of Sabbat alignments works well for many Witches, but for those who live in northern climates with cold, long winters, it doesn't *quite* line up exactly with how the seasons are experienced. In these regions, the New Moon, as a symbol of the end of darkness and the beginning of new life, is actually more closely aligned with Imbolc, which is the Sabbat celebrating the first stirrings of Spring.

Therefore, many Witches align the Moon's quarter marks with the Earth-based Sabbats instead. This shifts the system by a half-season, but still represents the overall timing and feel of the changes in the climate and landscape where they live.

In this framework, the Full Moon aligns with the cross-quarter day of Lughnasa (also Lammas), which is the first of the three harvest festivals. Given that "harvest" is a theme of the Full Moon, this makes as much sense as pairing the Full Moon with the Summer Solstice.

Furthermore, the Dark Moon period then falls between Yule and Imbolc—from late December through the end of January, when many start to feel as if the Winter will never end!

Depending on where you live, one of these alignment systems may make more intuitive sense than the other. Those who live near the equator, for example, may prefer the solar alignments, since the changes in seasons are not as noticeable as they are in the regions closer to the North and South poles.

For the purposes of this guide, however, we will use the Earth-based alignments as shown in the following table, since they more accurately reflect the seasons in the regions where Western Witchcraft originated.

Moon Phase	Sabbat	Season
New	Imbolc (Feb 2)	Late Winter / Early Spring
Waxing Crescent	Spring Equinox (Ostara)	Spring
Waxing Half	Beltane (May 1)	Late Spring / Early Summer
Half to Full (Gibbous)	Summer Solstice (Litha)	Summer
Full	Lughnasa / Lammas (Aug 1)	Late Summer / Early Autumn
Full to Half (Gibbous)	Autumn Equinox (Mabon)	Autumn
Waning Half	Samhain (Oct 31)	Late Autumn / Early Winter
Waning Crescent	Winter Solstice (Yule)	Winter
Dark	(none)	(period between Yule and Imbolc)

So how do these correspondences between Moon phases and the Sabbats and seasons affect magical work? Depending on how you approach your own magical practice, there are a number of possibilities.

You might, for example, use them to choose an auspicious timing for a particular spell. If you're seeking to draw romantic love into your life—or to reenergize an existing relationship—you know that the waxing phase is the best time to work. This gives you a window of two weeks.

But what if you want to narrow it down further? Take a look at the Sabbat correspondences and you'll notice that Beltane, a Sabbat associated with love and lust, falls at the waxing Half Moon. Why not choose this date, drawing on the bright, playful energies of Beltane as you send your magical intention for love out into the Universe?

Of course, many Wiccans make use of correspondences between magical purposes and the days of the week. In this system, Friday is the most ideal for working love spells, which may or may not line up with the waxing Half Moon.

If the waxing Half does fall on a Friday, then you're looking at a truly stellar alignment for your particular goal! If it falls on a different day, then you will need to use your intuition to decide on the best timing for your love spell. As always when it comes to magic, do what works best for you.

Another approach is to simply incorporate the *feeling* of the corresponding season into your magical work. For example, in a spell for love you can imagine the delicious warming up of late Spring / early Summer—that promising preview of the warmth and lushness of Summer coming into full swing—and use the feelings created by those thoughts to fuel your magic.

And if you're the type to create your own spells from scratch, you can use the corresponding season and/or Sabbat as inspiration for deciding on ingredients. For example, there are tons of herbs associated with romantic love, but which ones are at their peak during the Beltane season? Which are commonly used at Beltane celebrations?

Doubling up on your correspondences in this way can make your magic incredibly potent!

ALIGNING WITH GROWTH CYCLES

Another creative framework for magical correspondences aligns the phases of the Moon with the stages of the life cycle of plants.

Although there is obviously a lot of variation between different kinds of plants—flowers, shrubs, trees, herbs, wild vs. cultivated plant life, etc.—a basic pattern is observed in the workings of the world of vegetation.

With a few exceptions (like mosses, ferns and mushrooms), every plant begins as a seed. Given the right conditions of soil, water and light, the seed will root and begin to grow. As it reaches upward toward the sun, leaves begin to develop, followed by buds which become flowers.

The flowers are pollinated—by bees, moths, butterflies, bats, or wind, depending on the species—which produces the fruit of the plant. The fruit contains the seeds that will start the next cycle of growth.

(Note that the term "fruit" is being loosely applied here, and doesn't necessarily refer to something we would eat. A pinecone, for example, contains the seeds needed to grow new pine trees. Nuts are also considered fruits in this growth cycle model.)

Once the fruit has reached its ripest point, it will either be eaten by an animal or drop to the ground. Either way, the seeds will ultimately find their way back into the soil, beginning the cycle all over again.

When we view the growth cycle and the lunar cycle together, we can align the two quite symmetrically, like this:

Moon Phase	Growth Cycle Phase
New	Seed
Waxing Crescent	Root
Waxing Half	Leaf
Half to Full (Gibbous)	Bud
Full	Flower

Moon Phase	Growth Cycle Phase
Full to Half (Gibbous)	Fruit
Waning Half	Harvest
Waning Crescent	Compost
Dark	(Rest)

How are these correspondences meaningful to magic? Aside from providing us with another framework for viewing the phases of the Moon, the life cycle of plants serves as a great metaphor for the co-creative nature of magical manifestation.

Too often, beginning practitioners of magic will work spells for big goals and then sit around wondering why they didn't meet the partner of their dreams or become a millionaire this week. For one thing, the Law of Attraction—which is a big part of magic—states that you get what you think about, so if you're constantly focusing on how you still haven't seen your dream come true, that's exactly what you'll continue to experience.

It's important to direct your thoughts to the manifestation *itself*, not the lack of it. More to the point, however, is the need to do your part in the co-creation of what you seek to manifest. If you learn to think of yourself as a magical "gardener," you will get a clearer sense of how and why your participation is a key component.

Whether we intend to grow flowers, herbs, vegetables, or trees, there is a balance between the actions we need to take, and the transformative processes that Nature alone is responsible for. We do the planting, the watering and nurturing, but the creation of leaf, bud, flower and fruit is all Nature's doing.

When our manifestation has fully culminated, it's up to us to either reap the fruit or let it over-ripen and drop to the ground. The composting remains of whatever we don't use are naturally designed to propagate new life the following season, but we can give this process great assistance and direction by tending the soil, weeding out what is unwanted, and preparing the garden for its winter rest.

Furthermore, the growth cycle illustrates the role of *timing* in magic, not only as it relates to the energies of Moon phases, but also in terms of how manifestation actually occurs as it moves from the invisible plane to the physical plane. Just as each stage of the growth cycle has its particular purpose in the overall enterprise of plant creation, magical manifestation happens in stages.

Most often, the initial developments taking place are not visible to the eye, just as a seed takes root under the surface of the soil. And even as the manifestation begins to emerge, it may not immediately be recognized for what it is, just as most seedlings tend to resemble each other, no matter what species of plant they are. For those with untrained eyes, it takes some time before they've grown enough to be distinguishable from other plants.

The beginnings of our manifestations can be like this—a chance conversation with an acquaintance that turns out to be a tip on a new job possibility, or a run of what *seems* to be bad luck (a fender bender, a delayed flight) that puts us in the path of our next true love. Most realized goals can be traced back to a winding chain of actions and events that seemed unrelated or insignificant until the manifestation became clear.

So if your magic is to succeed, it's not enough to simply plant a seed of intention. You'll need to nurture it. You'll need to be willing to leave your house, get out and meet people, and yes, maybe even buy a lottery ticket (though if you're convinced that your only chance at wealth is through a game with incredibly stiff odds, you won't be open to other, unseen possibilities).

You'll also need to practice being alert to subtle nudges from the Universe—i.e., your intuition—that may be trying to show you the seedlings of your intentions poking up through the soil.

Finally, you'll have to have patience, since no matter what actions you take, Nature works on its own schedule.

Be aware of the difference between what you can do and what is strictly up to the Universe, and be willing to let the manifestation unfold according to divine timing. Of course, it's true that some manifestations *do* happen very quickly, just as some plants literally do spring up overnight. But even these still started out as tiny seeds, hidden from view.

PUTTING IT ALL TOGETHER: THE LUNAR PHASES

As you can see, there are many ways to view the Moon's cycle when it comes to magic.

It begins with the understanding of waxing and waning energies, which correspond to the rising and ebbing tides. Adding the seasons and Sabbats to this framework integrates the magical energies of the Wheel of the Year into the lunar cycle. The Earth energy is further intensified by the growth cycle alignments, providing a microcosm, or inner "wheel," of connection with Nature.

Of course, not everyone will resonate with these approaches, as everyone's magical practice is unique and personal to them. However, those who do incorporate two or more of these systems of correspondence find that they come to a far more intuitive relationship with the process of manifestation than they had before.

Now we'll take a deeper look at the lunar cycle, with an eye for how the energies of each phase can help you shape your magic. We'll examine how each of the seasonal and growth cycle alignments can inform your choices in terms of goals to work for, and how you approach your spellwork.

For those who work with aspects of the Goddess, individual deities particularly suited for each particular Moon phase are also included, though please note that these are just a few examples, and that there is plenty of room for overlap between adjacent phases. In other words, goddesses who align with the waxing Crescent Moon are also suitable for other phases of the waxing half of the cycle, etc.

Utilizing these correspondence systems to help structure your magical practice will definitely enhance your spellwork, but it can also help you zero in on the goals that are most likely to be achieved at any given time. This is very helpful during those times when you want to set intentions for everything under the Sun and don't know where to start!

The discussion below outlines a trajectory of sorts for the manifestation process. However, it's important to note here that many, if not most magical goals are realized over a longer stretch of time than just one lunar cycle—especially large and significant ones.

For example, if you're intending to start a family, you're obviously not going to give birth to a child in two weeks' time. Likewise, it would very rarely be a good idea to get married at the Full Moon to someone you just met at the waxing Half-Moon!

However, many simple, short-term goals can be realized in one lunar cycle, and many long-term goals see increments of progress during these times. And you can learn to see the work of the waning phase—releasing what isn't wanted or no longer serves you—as part of the process of manifesting what you do want, as we will see below.

But regardless of how any given magical intention turns out, if you make a practice of working according to lunar rhythms, you will be strengthening your sixth-sense connection to the Universal energies, and enhancing your magic as a result.

NEW MOON

The New Moon marks the very earliest beginnings of the lunar cycle. After a period of darkness, with no source of light in the night sky, the tiniest sliver of the Moon's surface emerges. It's not yet big enough to be visible to the naked eye, but it can still be felt, energetically, by many who are attuned to lunar rhythms.

Just as Imbolc marks the first stirrings of new life beneath the still-cold ground, the New Moon extends a promise of new things to come.

This is the seed-time of the growth cycle—all the potential of a new manifestation is still contained within a small packet of highly charged energy, invisible to us as it remains buried in the soil.

This is a good time for dreaming of what you wish to create in your life. Perhaps you don't know exactly what you want it to look like, but taking some time to imagine how you will feel once it has manifested will guide you toward a more specific vision as the month goes on.

For example, if you want to get a new job, but don't have a clear sense of where or in what field you'd like to work, use the New Moon as a time to open up to various possibilities—including those you haven't consciously thought of—and tune in to your intuition about which ones feel the most alive to you. Work a spell that asks for help in clarifying your employment goals, or invite a number of potential offers to come your way so you can make decisions from a highly empowered place.

Traditionally, magic aimed at initiating new projects and ventures is favored at this time, but anything involving attracting or increasing what you desire is appropriate here. It's also a good time for formalizing any intentions aimed at self-improvement, whether it be an exercise plan or a resolution to learn more about a particular topic.

It's helpful to keep in mind that New Moon spells aren't really about *instant* manifestation. They're about new beginnings, initiating actions that will bear fruit down the road. We plant the seeds, water them gently, and remain patient as they begin to germinate.

Many Witches work their spells as close as possible to the exact time of the New Moon, or just after, as this is thought to be the most potent time to harness the magical energies of this phase. Others prefer to cast New Moon spells during daylight hours, since at this point in the cycle the Moon rises and sets with the Sun.

Of course, you may not have the luxury of following either of these strategies, depending on your daily schedule. If this is the case, don't let it worry you. Just do your best to work on the actual day (or night) of the New Moon or no more than one day after, if you want to align your work with these particular energies, which will continue to influence events throughout the waxing phase.

Goddesses: Diana (Roman), Artemis (Greek), Astarte (Phoenician)

WAXING CRESCENT

Beginning with the day after the New Moon, and over the next few days, the Crescent Moon becomes more and more noticeable in the sky. The dream-time is turning more outwardly toward manifestation as the seedlings we have planted start taking root in the soil.

In fact, many intuitive people find that as the Moon grows brighter, their actual dreams become clearer and easier to understand, as the Universe is responding to the intentions we've been sending out. In the way that Spring begins to make itself known through the sudden appearance of buds and blossoms on the trees, our attention at the Crescent Moon is drawn to the subtle, yet distinct changes happening in our midst.

The crescent is a symbol of the Triple Goddess, envisioned by Wiccans as the shining cup of her hand, holding within her palm the potential of the Universe. The Goddess is coming into her Maiden role at this time, her youthful energy full of the promise of blessings to come.

This phase is the ideal time for taking action in the direction of our goals—actually beginning, on the physical plane, the projects we've intended for on the spiritual plane. The energy here is one of action and projecting our intentions outward into the Universe.

This can mean relatively small steps, such as establishing a routine of checking job listings, or contacting people you know can assist you with whatever it is you're seeking to manifest. Be willing to meet new people and/or vary your usual routine in order to allow new possibilities to come into your awareness. Watch for opportunities related to your goal to show up during this time, and be sure to take advantage of them, as doing so confirms to the Universe that you truly do want what you've been intending for.

This is how we root our manifestations—by taking the individual steps toward our goal as they present themselves. Just as the Spring unfolds little by little, yet steadily over each passing day, so do the circumstances that lead to your success.

Magic during the Crescent Moon continues to be related to attraction and increase, but the energy begins to pick up the pace and move things into a somewhat more defined focus.

Be willing to revisit the seed of intention you planted at the New Moon and evaluate how it may seem to be taking shape. Work spells to strengthen your resolve to see things through, and to draw even more assistance from the Universe in the days to come.

Spellwork regarding creativity, business, and financial matters in general is favored at this time, as this is a fortuitous time to begin new ventures and step out into the unknown. Truly, anything you wish to draw to you is a good area of focus now.

If you have a lot of inspired ideas and are unsure where to start, sit with each one and tune into your intuition. Which has the most active energy behind it when you think of it? Try starting there.

You can also ask the Maiden for guidance in selecting and focusing on your goal. Those who like to work when the Moon is up can cast spells from midmorning until the hour after sundown.

Goddesses: All Maiden goddesses, such as Aphrodite (Greek), Aine (Irish), Idunn (Norse)

WAXING HALF

Continuing its outward expansion, the Moon finishes out its first quarter and reaches the midpoint between New and Full.

This phase corresponds to the late Spring / early Summer season celebrated at Beltane. There is a somewhat more fiery aspect to the energy here as the pace of growth quickens and activities are ramping up. The Beltane holiday takes the loving, co-creative relationship between the God and Goddess as its theme, and this energy can be harnessed not just for love or romance, but for any goals that involve people coming together to create something new or enhance an existing creation.

Alternatively, if your goal does not include collaborating with others, you may find yourself in more consistent co-creation with the

Universe itself, discovering your "groove" as you continue to allow new opportunities related to your goal to flow into your experience.

At this point on the Wheel of the Year, those who live in northern climates see the trees suddenly coming to life as their new leaves transform the landscape. Likewise, in the growth cycle, the Half Moon aligns with the sprouting of leaves, which serve as a plant's "power station" by converting sunlight to fuel. This is the indication that this new life, which began as a seed, truly means to stick around.

It's an ideal time to begin building your own infrastructure related to your magical goals, whether this means creating more detailed plans, following through on initial opportunities, or gathering support from those who can be of assistance. The main idea here is a heightened emphasis on growth, and nurturing your newly-sprouted intention. What can you do to harness the increasing push of energy coming from the Moon to fuel your progress?

If you're not experiencing any evidence of manifestation yet, there may be various factors at play. Are you staying in touch with your intuition, and paying attention to subtle nudges from the Universe? Are unexpected circumstances or changes occurring in your daily life?

Remember that sometimes, occurrences that seem inconvenient or annoying in the moment turn out to be steps on the path to realizing the goal, though we have no way of knowing it yet. Do your best to be at peace and trust the Universe to work out the "how" and the "when" of your manifestation. If you are attached to specific expectations, you may be blocking the ability of what you desire to come into your life.

Magical work at the waxing Half Moon is generally related to gaining or strengthening partnerships with others, whether they be friends, romantic interests, or business associates. Improving physical health and general well-being is also favored now.

You may also feel guided to "boost" any spellwork begun at the New Moon, perhaps by lighting a candle to add new energy to the existing working, creating a luck charm with your goal in mind, or simply by visualizing the manifestation with increasing clarity. It's not too late to set brand-new intentions, either, as there's still time between now and the Full Moon for the waxing energy to influence your magic.

This is still a time of powerful potential. Midday to midnight are the hours to work with if you're timing your spells with the Moon's presence in the sky.

Goddesses: Athena (Greek), Bast (Egyptian), Rhiannon (Welsh)

WAXING HALF TO FULL (GIBBOUS)

Shortly after reaching the Half, or 2nd-quarter mark, it becomes clear that the Moon is nearly Full. People tend to notice the Moon more during this phase, as it emerges just after sunset and rises later into the night sky.

Energies begin to intensify at this time, with heightened emotions and sharper instincts manifesting at the conscious level. Many people experience an increase in precognitive dreams and intuitive "hits" in the days leading up to the Full Moon, and some have more trouble sleeping than at any other time of the lunar month.

The waxing gibbous Moon corresponds to the weeks surrounding the Summer Solstice, when the trees and other vegetation are practically exploding with lushness and the newborn animals begin to gain independence.

Magical intentions set at the New Moon and tended throughout the waxing phase are about to come into fruition, provided we continue to believe in our success. The Goddess is now coming into her Mother aspect, her womb growing larger as the Moon grows with each passing hour.

This sense of manifestation being just on the verge of arrival is represented by the bud stage of the growth cycle, which the waxing gibbous phase corresponds to. The vision of a soon-to-unfold flower is a powerful metaphor for the delicious anticipation of new creations coming forth. It is also a good lesson in the importance of patience and trust in divine timing, as you cannot hurry the flower's process.

In terms of spellwork, no further direct action on our part is truly necessary at this point, as the flower will develop on its own, but we can use this stretch of days to make preparations for the upcoming Full Moon celebration, when we will welcome the unfolding of our intentions. Of course, if your daily life presents you with opportunities or clear steps to take related to your goal, by all means move forward with them!

Magically, this is considered to be an "all-purpose" phase, but the work should still be harnessing projective energy and focus on increase and drawing what you desire into your life. If you feel guided to, you may want to give a final boost of energy to any work begun at any point in the waxing phase.

Be sure to also take time to note any progress that has become apparent so far, no matter how subtle. Give yourself a pat on the back for any and all actions you've taken in pursuit of your goal, regardless of whether they seem to have had any effect yet. Continue to pay attention to your dreams and your intuitive hunches for messages you may be receiving from the Universe related to your desires.

As for new intentions, the waxing gibbous Moon has a "quickening" energy to it, so spells cast now will manifest swiftly, particularly if they are simple and well-focused. This energy is best harnessed after sundown, and before the first stirrings of dawn.

Goddesses: Nuit (Egyptian), Asteria (Greek), Luna (Roman)

FULL MOON

The Full Moon is the most powerful phase of the entire lunar cycle. Even people who don't believe in magic are able to recognize that something is energetically "different" at the Full Moon, as they experience strong emotions, erratic behavior in themselves or others, or strange sleep patterns.

Those who do understand magic are in an excellent position to take advantage of these lunar energies and bring their desires into physical reality at this time. Many Witches find that the day of the Full Moon is the most magically potent day of the month, and may save spellwork related to particularly important goals for this occasion. Divination can also be particularly successful at this time, as can efforts to improve psychic abilities.

The Full Moon represents absolute abundance and the full promise of the growth cycle. This is the flowering stage in the world of plant life—the flourish of beauty confirming that the fruit is on its way. The Mother aspect of the Triple Goddess is in her full power now, lending her nurturing and tending energies to our manifestations in progress.

This phase also corresponds with Lughnasa, the first of the three harvest festivals on the Wheel of the Year and the cross-quarter day between Summer and Autumn. Agriculturally speaking, this is the harvest with the most promise, as we are just beginning to reap the benefits of what we planted at the beginning of the cycle, yet we know that the bulk of the bounty is yet to come.

In keeping with this harvest theme, many Wiccans and other Witches make a point of expressing gratitude in their Full Moon celebrations. You may wish to write a list of all that has benefited you over the past month and thank the Universe (or the Goddess and/or the God, or whatever concept or identity you connect with in terms of a "higher power") for these blessings. Doing so before making any new magical requests is a great way to both honor the Full Moon theme of abundance and raise your vibrational frequency to an optimal state before sending out your new intention.

As for the intentions you began this lunar cycle with, use this phase to once again acknowledge the progress made thus far, to clarify what it is you want to see happen next, and to realign yourself with the energies of accomplishing your goal.

Often, the co-creative nature of manifestation means that you may experience a "false start" or two, which helps you refine your vision of what is ultimately the best outcome. For example, maybe you landed an interview for a job, only to discover that the company is not a good fit for you. You can use this experience to help you visualize, to an even more specific degree, the career circumstances that will suit you best.

Any and all magical purposes are favored at the Full Moon. If you can't decide on a specific goal, however, you can try letting magical timing be your guide. As mentioned in Part One, each Full Moon is traditionally linked with the season, the month, and/or the Zodiac sign in which it occurs. So you can choose according to seasonal correspondences—working for material abundance on a Full Moon in

Autumn, for example, or banishing health problems on a Winter Full Moon.

Alternatively, you might work with the Zodiac sign that the Full Moon is occurring in, or with the current Sun sign. For example, spells related to communication or travel are good to work during Gemini, while Leo is a time to work for love, children, and vacations. (You can find more information about these systems in the Tables of Correspondence at the end of this guide.)

If you decide to adopt a regular practice of linking the Full Moon to the Zodiac, try to be consistent with your choice of alignments, for better overall momentum. In other words, if you work a Full Moon "Gemini" spell when the Sun is in Gemini, you should then use Cancer as your magical guide at the next Full Moon, rather than switching to the sign the Moon is in.

Of course, there are no hard-and-fast rules surrounding any of this—you should always work for what you feel are the most pressing goals, regardless of the seasonal or Zodiac correspondences.

As with the New Moon, many Witches try to work as closely as possible to the exact moment that the Moon becomes Full for maximum magical advantage. However, this moment often occurs at midday or early in the morning, which can be pretty inconvenient, especially for covens holding an Esbat!

Since working under moonlight is also an ideal condition for magic, it can be just as effective to cast your spells several hours later, once the sun has set and the Moon has risen, or else the night before it turns Full. In fact, some would argue that the window of time is even wider, given that the lunar energies surrounding the Full Moon begin to intensify up to three days beforehand and linger for at least two days afterward.

Although it's widely agreed that it's better to work before the Moon turns Full than afterward, this is really entirely up to your degree of focused intention and your circumstances. There may be situations when you just aren't able to time your work according to ideal conditions—don't let that prevent you from celebrating the Full Moon and casting your spell with enthusiasm!

Goddesses: All Mother goddesses, such as Arianrhod (Welsh), Danu (Irish), Isis (Egyptian), Selene (Greek)

FULL TO WANING HALF (GIBBOUS)

Within a few days after the Full Moon, the strong lunar energies have clearly begun to recede, ebbing like the ocean waves just after high tide. Now begins the waning half of the cycle, as the Moon starts to disappear gradually into shadow.

The Autumn Equinox marks this turning toward the dark time of year, and the days become noticeably shorter than just weeks ago. The Mother Goddess has reached the point of full maturity along her path and now progresses onward to greater and greater wisdom.

The harvest is in full swing now as Autumn's bounty is reaped from the fields. The fully ripened fruit is gathered and put to use. What can't be used is left to drop to the ground where it will feed the animals and the soil.

This is a time to harvest the fruit of our magical efforts, which includes affirming and giving thanks for any manifestations that have arrived or are on the horizon. Be sure to enjoy everything that has come into your life, and celebrate your efforts on both the physical and non-physical planes.

This is also the time to release the energy of outward action, and align with the energy of inward reflection. Let go of any specific spellwork that has yet to come into fruition. This doesn't mean you should give up on your goals—just release any attachments you have to outcomes from this particular spell.

It may be that there is a larger timeline for the manifestation to occur than you'd like, but this is where patience and trust in Universal timing comes in. In the meantime, you can take advantage of the waning energies of the lunar cycle to make some very beneficial changes in your life.

Eliminating negative energies and experiences is the governing principle of magic during the waning Moon. Spellwork aimed at overcoming obstacles, resolving conflicts, and removing causes of illness is favored at this time. Looking within and examining our inner landscape brings about clarity, and can help us identify where we might make more effective choices around recurring issues, both in our spellwork and in our daily lives.

Think of this work in terms of the harvest—we sort through what we've brought about and discard anything that doesn't serve us. What we let go of is released back to the Earth and ultimately transformed into new life.

Generally, this is a metaphorical suggestion for doing inner work on the level of the psyche, but it can also apply literally to cleaning and clearing. So if you've got a cluttered closet or any other area of your home that's been needing a good purge, this is an excellent time to get it done. Clear out the old and make room for the new—you may be surprised by how much your energy and mood improve after a good clutter-clearing session!

If you're still preoccupied by a goal that hasn't been realized during this time, shift your focus to one of banishing obstacles and releasing resistance—including any resistance to the fact that it hasn't yet manifested. Remember that you get what you focus on, so if you're having trouble envisioning your manifestation without feeling anxious or disappointed, work a spell for releasing those negative feelings and attachments, since they are not serving you.

As the Moon wanes, the obstacles, problems, and negative thought patterns you're experiencing will also recede. As with the Full Moon, working magic at night when the Moon is actually visible is ideal.

Goddesses: Demeter (Greek), Ceres (Roman), Freya (Norse)

WANING HALF

Just as the waxing Half Moon is a time of ramping up the projective, active energies of growth, the waning Half is accompanied by an increase in the receptive, passive energies of release. The Moon rises later and later with each passing night, with less and less illumination.

This is the harvest phase of the growth cycle—no more new growth will occur until the next Spring begins, so it's time to gather any last remaining fruits of this season's labor. This phase also corresponds with the third and final harvest festival, Samhain, which is when we make our preparations for the dark, cold Winter months.

This is not a somber time, however (although for those who deeply dislike the cold, it can seem like it!). Witches embrace both the light and the dark—as well as the heat and the cold—as equal parts of the whole of our experience on Earth. So while the focus of our magic may be on the less fun or joyful aspects of life—dealing with the unwanted, breaking unhealthy habits, etc.—we can appreciate the happiness that such work will ultimately bring into our lives.

As mentioned above, spellwork during the waning Moon is aimed at banishing and/or releasing negative influences and circumstances. Depending on how you view your life, you may have a fairly long list of things that fall into these categories! So how do you choose where to start?

For some, the process of deciding what to tackle at this time can feel overwhelming and even lead to despair. But there's no need to let the tricky work of addressing difficult issues get you down. For one thing, you're never expected to clear up all negativity from your life in one fell swoop! The work of removing what you don't want is similar to the work of attracting what you do want—your focus can't be on all things at the same time.

Happily, there will always be another two weeks of waning lunar energy to harness during the Moon's next cycle. With this in mind, you can make some wise decisions about your magical aims by taking one of the following approaches.

First, is there anything going on with you that needs immediate attention, such as a case of the flu, or a mechanical issue with your car? If so, the waning Half Moon is a perfect time to work a spell for releasing and resolving these problems.

If there are no immediately pressing issues, then simply identify a goal that feels achievable to you at this time. Perhaps it's releasing an addictive relationship with a particular food, or escaping unnecessary interactions with an annoying coworker. For bigger, more challenging problems, it's advisable to wait until the Crescent or even Dark Moon to set your intentions.

Many Witches find that the further the Moon wanes, the stronger its power to banish, remove, and release the unwanted. So use the first half of the waning phase for somewhat lighter work around release and removal, and use your successes to fuel your energy and confidence for the more powerful magic you want to work at the end of this lunar cycle.

Night is still the best time for casting your spells, and you can still catch the moon in the night sky for a few more evenings, before it begins to rise quite late.

Goddesses: the Cailleach (Celtic), Nepthys (Egyptian), Hella (Norse)

WANING CRESCENT

The waning Crescent Moon is the final point on the lunar cycle when the Moon is still visible at all, before it disappears completely into its Dark days.

This Crescent corresponds to the time of the Winter Solstice, or Yule—the festival of light that serves to remind us that new light, and new life, will come again at Winter's end. It also corresponds to the compost phase of the growth cycle—when the remaining, decaying plant matter is transformed into nutrients in the soil for the next generation of life to make use of.

Energetically, this is a very powerful time for conquering negative circumstances through release and removal. Magical work related to protection, banishing, and binding troublesome people or situations is favored now.

However, be careful not to adopt an attitude of conflict or battle when it comes to the issues you're working to resolve. If you see yourself as being engaged in an active fight, you will most likely reinforce the negative conditions, rather than releasing them.

For example, if your goal is to remove a major illness, keep your focus on how you will feel when you are well, rather than on "fighting" how you feel now. This is another instance where keeping the Law of Attraction in mind can really help you shape your magic. If you feel inclined, ask for assistance from the Crone Goddess, whose energies of wisdom and clear thinking are best suited for dealing with endings and removal.

It's also useful to keep the metaphor of composting in mind here. Although what we are releasing is not desirable or useful to us, it can be transformed into neutral or even beneficial energy in the larger world.

If you think about it, you don't resent the existence of a banana peel or a rotten tomato simply because you can't eat them! They may be unpleasant to the senses, but that doesn't mean they are inherently "bad." In fact, they can be turned to good if they are allowed to decompose and therefore nourish the soil.

Similarly, everything we release has had its own purpose—including conflicts, illness, and other challenges. What we learn from our struggles is just as useful as what we enjoy about our successes.

For example, let's say you're working to recover from a painful breakup of a romantic relationship. You might want to start with a spell to release your attachments to the past, and then move on to work related to healing the feelings that are hurting you right now.

However, don't put any energy into resentment about what happened, or fear of what's coming next. Work for acceptance of things as they are, and know that this experience will help you to navigate the next relationship along your path.

If you need to protect yourself from a person who is a harmful influence in your life, you can do a binding spell to keep them out of your way, but don't wish them harm in return. For one thing, this isn't necessary for your spellwork to succeed—in fact, negative intent will most likely lead your spell to backfire.

When it comes to conflicts of any kind, a good general rule of thumb is to work for the best outcome for all involved, rather than trying to "win" or prove that you're right.

Waning magic is still ideal to work at night, but timing to align with the Moon's presence in the sky is tricky, since this Crescent won't rise until 3 a.m. That's a difficult time for most people to pull off any spellwork (but if you're able to, go for it)! If you're an early riser, you might try working just before dawn, instead, as the Moon will still be climbing in the sky at that point.

Goddesses: All Crone goddesses, such as Hecate (Greek), Cerridwen (Welsh), the Morrigan (Irish)

DARK MOON

During the final stretch of days before the Moon turns New again, it cannot be seen at all in the sky. This is often experienced as a quiet, yet fairly strange time, when energy levels fluctuate, logic becomes "fuzzy," and progress toward our goals can seem to be at a standstill.

In the Wheel of the Year alignments, this phase has no season or Sabbat, as we are dealing with the Moon's absence rather than its presence. However, it can be thought of as the period of time between the Winter Solstice and Imbolc, which in northern climates is often called the "dead" of Winter.

In the growth cycle alignments, the Dark Moon corresponds to the period of rest between growing cycles—a time to let the soil be, so that its nutrients can be replenished before it's time to plant new seeds.

This phase is also known as the "Balsamic Moon" in many traditions. The origins of the word "balsamic" are rooted in concepts related to healing, soothing, and restoring.

Many Witches use this period in exactly this way, refraining from actively working magic while they relax and refresh their energy for the next waxing phase. This can be a time for reading up on new magical techniques and approaches, as well as practicing divination and meditation.

In some traditions, the Dark Moon is the ideal time for past life regression, for the purpose of finding answers and insights regarding current challenges. Communicating with ancestors and loved ones in the spirit world can be especially productive during these days.

Abstaining from spellwork is certainly not mandatory, however. Plenty of people find the Dark Moon to be the best time for magic related to closure, or bringing things full circle.

We are still in the realm of the Crone, so this is a powerful time for releasing any karmic patterns that crop up again and again in your life, such as those related to lack, abandonment, betrayal, etc.

There is a destructive potential to the energy now that can be harnessed for these purposes. As always, remember to focus your intent on eliminating the situation itself, rather than aiming negativity at any people involved.

If you're timing your magic with the Moon's presence in the sky (invisible though it may be), work spells between three in the morning and three in the afternoon. And if you're having a difficult time for any reason during this phase, remember that the New Moon, and therefore a new beginning, is just around the corner.

Goddesses: All Crone goddesses

CHARTING YOUR OWN COURSE

Hopefully, you now have a clearer appreciation for the ever-shifting lunar energies associated with the cycles of the Moon and their magical implications.

Witches have long known that when we work with these rhythms of waxing and waning, we can align our magic with the projective and receptive currents of the tidal flow of the Universe. We learn to honor the roles of both creation and destruction in the cycles of Nature, and recognize that each has its part to play in the larger process of manifestation.

By choosing to follow the path of the Moon as an integral part of your magical practice, you are stepping into a rich tradition, begun long ago by our ancestors who implicitly understood the inherent power of Earth's celestial companion. Over time, as you gain experience with this approach to magical living, you will find your own understanding of these lunar energies setting roots within your psyche, and flourishing during every phase of the cycle.

It's important to note that this does take time—don't expect to be completely in tune with the Moon's energy every single day starting tomorrow. In fact, don't even expect yourself to follow the path outlined above for an entire lunar cycle on your first try.

You can certainly aim for that if you wish to, but be sure not to let yourself get discouraged if you lose track of which phase the Moon is in for a few days. Especially for less experienced Witches, it may take a few full cycles—or more—before you start becoming aware of the more subtle shifts in lunar energy.

Most people can feel the New Moon and Full Moon fairly easily when they tune in, but other points of the cycle tend to take awhile to detect on a sixth-sense level. If you're just starting out on this journey, and especially if you're new to magic, you may want to decide to focus on just the waxing phase at first.

Make a point of honoring the New Moon and spend some time identifying and visualizing your goals. Plan for some related spellwork to be done at the waxing Crescent or the waxing Half. Take note of any results—including hunches, signs, and potential developments— and stay open to more as the Moon continues to wax.

Celebrate the Full Moon and reflect on your experience of following the lunar path up to this point. Don't forget to congratulate yourself for having come this far! Then, decide how you'd like to approach the waning phase.

If it's starting to feel overwhelming, or like a chore rather than an enlightening experiment, take a break and plan to focus on the waning phase the next time it comes around. That's the beauty of cycles—they never end, so there will always be another opportunity for learning and growing in your practice.

WORKING FOR LARGER GOALS OVER SEVERAL CYCLES

As acknowledged above, many—if not most—manifestations have a longer timeline than one lunar cycle could ever allow for.

You're very unlikely to be able to apply for *and* get into college, build your dream house, or write a best-selling novel from start to finish within the two week waxing cycle. Even goals that could theoretically be realized in this time frame, such as landing a good job, may take longer for a variety of reasons.

Perhaps the job of your dreams is on its way, but the person currently in the position has yet to give their resignation notice. Or it could be that your ideal romantic match won't be moving to your city for another few months.

So don't conclude that your spellwork failed simply because the Full Moon has come and gone and you can't yet see the evidence of your success!

(Furthermore, don't assume that the days around the Full Moon are the only window of opportunity for manifestations to reveal themselves. Although the waning phase is traditionally a time to focus on releasing things from our lives, plenty of fortunate circumstances can, and do, come into our experience during this time as well.)

So what should you do with those larger intentions as the next New Moon comes around? Should you keep working spells for love, prosperity, career advancement, etc., during every lunar cycle until your goals are realized?

The answer really depends on how you go about it. If you're repeating the same spell over and over, then you're likely telling the Universe (and yourself) that you don't believe your prior efforts have set anything in motion, even though events and circumstances may very well be shaping up to bring you what you desire. This can set you up for an endless cycle of starting over, so that you're blocking any progress that would otherwise be making its way to you.

A wiser approach would be to experiment with different kinds of spellwork from Moon to Moon, still focusing on your goal but from the perspective of adding new and various layers of energy to the initial spell. For example, you might work a candle spell for financial abundance during the first cycle, and then create a charm for the same outcome during the next waxing Moon, which you can carry with you for the duration of two more lunar cycles.

Be sure to take note of any manifestations, no matter how small or seemingly insignificant, throughout the process. This can be a great way to develop your magical talent, explore new methods, and discover what kinds of spellwork suit you best.

Finally, keep in mind that larger, multi-cycle manifestations happen in steps.

If your goal is a new career, for example, you might first be prompted to enroll in some classes related to your desired field. Let that be your focus for one lunar cycle, working spells to boost your success in your new studies.

Next, you might focus on finding help polishing up your resume. Focusing on the individual steps not only helps you take action in the material world, but also helps you specify the focus of your magic as you patiently allow the larger goal—the brand-new, exciting and fulfilling job—to unfold according to right timing.

The same is true for waning Moon goals. If you're like most people, you probably aren't going to completely get over the end of a significant relationship all in one waning cycle. But you can work to release your emotional attachments and heal your grief one step at a time, allowing the rhythms of the lunar cycle to guide your journey.

Indeed, the Moon's never-ending cycles can provide a comforting and nurturing structure for us as we witness the unfolding of all of our manifestations, no matter how long they take to come to fruition.

GETTING CREATIVE WITH TIMING

There's one potential "glitch" in the system of working with lunar alignments that every Witch will encounter at one point or another—the inconvenience of unexpected obstacles.

In other words, what happens when your immediate needs are at odds with the current Moon phase?

What if you need to work a spell for fast cash for a car repair, or some other expense that simply won't wait until the Moon is waxing again? Or, what if there's a conflict that needs resolution, but it's only a few days after the waxing Crescent?

Does this mean there is no magical recourse available to you in these instances? Of course not!

First of all, the Moon phase alignments are guidelines, rather than absolute rules. They add tremendous power to your spellwork, but the

Universe is infinitely vast and infinitely capable of responding to your magical requests no matter where the Moon is in relation to the Earth.

So don't ever feel that your spell won't work at all because it's the wrong phase of the lunar cycle. As long as your energy is sufficiently focused on your intention—and if your need is great enough to warrant working against the lunar tides—then you will succeed.

However, it will help enormously if you can design your spellwork to be as compatible as possible with the current Moon phase, no matter the specific goal. Again, it's really all about how you approach your intention.

For example, let's say you're just chomping at the bit to work a prosperity spell, but the Moon is on the wane. Odds are that your strong desire to focus on this area of your life is coming from a sense of lack, or a belief that you never have enough money.

This is a great time for spellwork to release this "scarcity thinking," which, due to the Law of Attraction, is essentially the driving force behind all money woes.

In the case of the needed car repair, you can view the situation as an obstacle to be banished, rather than as a specific need for money. Remember, you never know *how* a manifestation might occur, so focusing on the outcome, rather than on the financial need, makes much magical sense during the waning Moon.

Feeling a need to release a relationship while the Moon is waxing? You can start with spellwork focused on building your inner strength and increasing your self-care, so that you'll have the courage and resolve it takes to make a clean break of it.

It's still recommended to wait for the waning Moon to do the actual breaking off, or releasing, but if you've been preparing during the waxing Moon by attracting the right frame of mind, you will be better able to bide your time until the lunar energies are in alignment with your goal.

As you can no doubt see by now, shaping your magic to harmonize with the Moon's movements around the Earth is an art that takes patience and practice. Working with the lunar energies of each phase of the cycle, and tailoring your spellwork to best align with either the waxing or waning currents, is not a skill you can learn overnight.

However, if you put in the time and the effort, you will certainly begin to see results in short order. It won't be long until you're moving naturally with the rhythms of the Moon, learning to relate intuitively to each phase of the cycle in equal turn.

Once you've gotten these basics down, then you'll be ready to have even more fun with the rare lunar events that come around just a few times a year (or less!), which we'll take a brief look at next.

BLUE MOONS AND LUNAR ECLIPSES

Although every Full Moon is a time of heightened magical power, there are two types of events that bring extra special energy to these lunar occasions: Blue Moons and Lunar Eclipses.

These rare occurrences often drum up plenty of attention within the mainstream world, but Witches are the ones who know how to harness their energy for magical success.

These two events differ in key ways. For instance, Blue Moons occur as a result of how we measure the solar year, while Lunar Eclipses are a function of the Earth's and Moon's orbits in space.

A Blue Moon is not actually blue and doesn't look any different from any other Full Moon, whereas a Lunar Eclipse can be quite noticeable, provided it occurs during nighttime hours.

Regardless of these differences, however, both of these lunar events are important to many Wiccans and other Witches, who make a point of observing them through ritual and spellwork on those rare occasions when they appear.

BLUE MOONS

You've no doubt heard the phrase "once in a Blue Moon" used to describe something that only happens very infrequently.

The origins of the term "Blue Moon" are thought to come from a few different possible sources, beginning with references going back to the 16th century and ultimately ending up in the titles of novels, songs, and even a flavor of ice cream.

Interestingly, the phrase initially referred to something that was completely impossible, used in the same way that people today might use "when pigs fly." However, there have in fact been documented cases of the Moon appearing blue in the sky, as a result of dust or smoke particles in the atmosphere from volcanoes and forest fires.

Of course, our modern concept of Blue Moons has nothing to do with the Moon's visual appearance, but rather with the Moon turning Full at an irregular time as measured by the yearly calendar—an "extra" Full Moon of sorts.

There are two different systems for identifying a Blue Moon. The first comes from farmer's almanacs of the 19th and early 20th centuries, which listed the Full Moons of each year using names borrowed from Native American traditions (many of which are now incorporated into Wiccan and other Pagan practices, as we saw in Part One).

Typically, there are three Full Moons in each season, or quarter, of the year—from the Winter Solstice to the Spring Equinox, for example.

When four Full Moons occurred in this period, the almanacs would call the third of the four a Blue Moon. These seasonal Blue Moons occur roughly every 2 to 3 years.

The second and more well-known type of Blue Moon is the second Full Moon of a calendar month. These occur with roughly every 32 to 33 months, and every 19 years or so we see two Blue Moons within one calendar year.

Most contemporary Witchcraft traditions around the Blue Moon observe the two-in-one-month version. But whether you consider the monthly or the seasonal Blue Moon to be the real deal (and why not go with both?), there's plenty of magical opportunity on these special occasions.

Many Wiccans view the Blue Moon as a time of heightened connection with the Goddess. Spells worked at this time are considered to have far more potency than typical Full Moon spells. Some Witches even believe that the effects of spellwork done at this time can have effects lasting until the next Blue Moon!

In particular, magic related to wisdom, love, and protection is effective on a Blue Moon, as are all forms of divination. And if you have any dreams that you have previously considered impossible to achieve, this is the perfect time to give spellwork a try!

LUNAR ECLIPSES

Less rare, but perhaps far more powerful than a Blue Moon is a Full Moon Lunar Eclipse, which happens generally twice a year (though some years may see three or more, depending on the circumstances).

Lunar Eclipses occur when the Earth's shadow blocks the light from the Sun, which would otherwise be illuminating the Moon.

There are three types of Eclipses—partial, penumbral, and total.

A partial Lunar Eclipse occurs when only part of the Moon enters the inner section of the Earth's shadow, called the umbra. The outer section of the shadow is the penumbra, and when the Moon passes only through this section it's called a penumbral Eclipse.

Total Lunar Eclipses occur when the Moon moves completely into the innermost, darkest part of the umbra, and these are the most visually stunning. Aside from seeming to almost disappear, the Moon can take on a vivid reddish hue during total Eclipses, depending on the atmospheric conditions.

In terms of magical energy, any of the three types are excellent occasions for extra special spellwork, but the total Lunar Eclipse is considered by many to be the most powerful lunar event of all.

Why is this? During a total Eclipse, the Moon appears to move through its entire lunar cycle in the span of just a few hours. As it moves through the Earth's shadow, it appears to wane, disappear, then reappear and wax again until Full.

This means that you can tap into each phase of the Moon's cycle in a brief period of time, rather than over the course of a month. You can do work for increase and decrease in one sitting if you like, or set new intentions for one aspect of your life while celebrating the culmination of another.

And if you're lucky enough to be able to actually watch the Eclipse in the night sky, well, that's about as magical as it gets! But don't be discouraged if you're not personally able to view it—the energetic benefits of the Eclipse are still available to you, if you wish to harness it through magical work.

Likewise, if you can perform your spells during the time of the actual Eclipse, whether or not it's visible in the sky, this is ideal, but if not, try to work after sundown, once the Full Moon has risen.

So what kind of magic is best to work during a Lunar Eclipse? As with any Full Moon, this is an all-purpose lunar phase, so anything you wish to work for is perfectly appropriate. However, many Witches find that a few specific areas are especially suited to Eclipse energy and spellwork related to these areas is particularly powerful.

Anything around healing, on all levels—physical, emotional, and spiritual—is good to intend for now, as is any work related to personal growth and/or spiritual development.

If you've been seeking to establish a relationship with a particular aspect of the God or Goddess, this is a good time to make offerings and spend time in meditation. Be open to subtle (and sometimes not-so-subtle) shifts in your energy as the deity responds to your request for contact. If the deity was primarily associated with the Moon in their original culture—such as Selene (Greek) or Toth (Egyptian)—this is highly likely to result in a powerful experience.

Finally, any magical activity that specifically honors or makes use of the Moon's energy, such as creating talismans and charging them in moonlight or taking a Full Moon ritual bath, has tremendous energetic effect during a Lunar Eclipse.

ENDLESS POSSIBILITIES

As we have now seen, the magic potential of the Moon is not limited to specific nights or special occasions. It's true that most of us feel its gravitational pull more during the New and Full Moons than at other times, and there are extremely powerful Blue Moons and Lunar Eclipses that amplify the lunar energy a few times per year.

But in actuality, every single day of the lunar cycle provides opportunities to align with the powerful energy of this celestial being. There is never a time when the Moon has no power—not even those days and nights when it seems to have disappeared completely.

Indeed, if you choose to, you can allow the Moon's energy to help you shape your approach to spellwork each and every day for the rest of your magical life!

So far, we have treated the practical aspects of lunar magic rather generally, in terms of choosing goals and tending your manifestations in harmony with the phases of the Moon. In Part Three, you'll find more specific, hands-on information to help you get on your way.

A few spells are included here, of course, as well as recipes for Moon-oriented magical oil blends; Tables of Correspondence for Moon-associated crystals, herbs, and flowers; methods for enhancing your personal connection with the Moon, and more. As always, keep yourself attuned to your intuition's responses to what you read. If a particular spell, method, or ingredient piques your interest, then you've found your best avenue to your next magical lunar adventure!

PART THREE

A LUNAR GRIMOIRE

A MISCELLANY
OF MOON MAGIC

Since at least the days of ancient Mesopotamia, magical information has been kept in texts that eventually came to be known as "grimoires." A grimoire is a book where you can find spells, rituals, incantations, recipes for potions, mystical symbols, keys to divination systems and just about anything else that fits under the "occult" umbrella.

The Wiccan version of the grimoire is, of course, the Book of Shadows, which is part of both coven and solitary traditions throughout the Wiccan world. You may already have one of your own, or you may be just beginning to compile information that will ultimately be included in your personal grimoire.

You can think of this final section of this guide as a short version of a "lunar" Book of Shadows. Each of the first four spells is focused on one of the four quarters of the lunar cycle, followed by spells for a Blue Moon and a Lunar Eclipse.

You'll also find a quick Table of Correspondence for spell ingredients associated with the Moon, for help in designing your own lunar spells. Suggested magical purposes to focus on during specific Moon phases and Zodiac locations can help you choose the most promising goals to work for at any given point in time.

Of course, there are other ways of working with the Moon beyond casting spells. To that end, pointers on lunar gardening, charging tools in moonlight, and creating your own Moon-associated magical oils and bath salts are included here. You'll also find a few suggestions for creating your own rituals of communing with the Moon, to help you deepen your spiritual connection to its energies.

Keep in mind, this is just a brief sample of the possibilities when it comes to lunar magic, but there's plenty here to get you started and inspire you to build your own practice.

A DAILY RITUAL
FOR GREETING THE MOON

The best way to develop your own personal relationship with the Moon is to interact with it directly, every day. Try integrating this brief ritual into your daily life for the entirety of one lunar cycle.

This is especially useful for those who are just starting to get acquainted with Moon magic, Wicca, or any other Nature-based spiritual path. It can take as little as two minutes, or longer if you like, depending on when you're able to work it into your schedule from day to day.

You will need to know when to expect the Moon to be visible in your area in order to plan. This information can easily be found online, and you can also refer to the rising and setting times chart at the end of Part Three for a rough guide.

For best results, stand outside under the Moon and gaze directly at it. If this isn't possible, look at it through a window.

Truly look at it. See if you notice any new details about its exact shape, its shadowy features, and its changing image as it disappears behind passing clouds, then reemerges.

Even if it's raining, you can still get a general sense of where the Moon is in the sky, so aim your focus there. If the Moon simply isn't in the sky at any point when you're awake, close your eyes and visualize it—as it appears in its current phase—as clearly as you can.

Spend some time silently communing with the lunar energy and when you feel ready, say the following words (or compose your own). If you're unable to do the ritual in private, you can say them silently.

"Today/tonight I greet you, Moon, with joy.
Thank you for your divine light,
your Goddess energy,
your sacred power.
I open myself to your mysteries
and welcome your eternal wisdom.
So let it be."

FOUR QUARTERS MOON
SPELL SERIES

This relatively simple spell is repeated throughout the lunar cycle, with variations appropriate to each phase.

While each of the four spells can certainly stand alone, there is a powerful advantage to working all of them for an entire lunar cycle, to establish an energetic pattern that aligns you with the Moon's rhythms.

You can tailor each working to your own practice by choosing your own combination of ingredients—feel free to substitute any of the suggested items below with other Moon-associated crystals, herbs, and flowers—and by stating your goals in your own words.

Each working might be focused on one aspect of the same overall goal, or the intentions for each spell may be unrelated to each other—it's all up to you.

You will need:

- 3 small pieces of moonstone, smoky quartz, and/or quartz crystal
- 1 teaspoon dried hibiscus, anise seed, lilac, and/or Irish moss
- 1 white tea light or spell candle
- 1 work candle (optional)

Instructions:

Light the work candle, if using.

Arrange the crystals in a triangle shape around the spell candle, and then use the herbs and/or flowers to create a circle encompassing the triangle.

Spend a few moments visualizing the Moon as it looks in its current phase. (You might want to place images of the Moon on your altar or work space for help.)

Now, visualize the outcome of manifesting your goal. When you feel ready, state your goal out loud, as if it has already come to be.

Light the spell candle, and seal the spell by saying the appropriate words below (or words of your own choosing):

1st quarter (New Moon):

> *"For my intention I plant these seeds,*
> *Knowing the Goddess will meet my needs."*

2nd quarter (Waxing Half):

> *"Day by day and night by night,*
> *My plans are growing with the light."*

3rd quarter (Full Moon):

> *"Abundant thanks for abundance blessed,*
> *and I know still more will manifest."*

4th quarter (Waning Half):

> *"I now release this _____ unwanted*
> *My mind is clear and my heart undaunted."*

Leave the candle to burn out on its own. Spell candles burn between 1-3 hours, while tea lights tend to last longer.

BLUE MOON
GOOD LUCK CHARM

Since the Blue Moon is indeed a rare occasion, you may as well make the most of it when it rolls around! Create a good luck charm infused with the lunar power of the Blue Moon, and keep it with you until the next one.

This spell draws on the energies of the color blue, which is infused with the qualities of peace, wisdom and protection, and often used in spellwork related to prosperity, health, and good luck.

You may want to add even more of this energy to the spell by decorating your altar or work space with blue fabrics, flowers, imagery, etc. and/or wearing blue yourself.

You will need:

- 1 blue votive or spell candle
- 7 small blue crystals, such as sodalite, lapis lazuli, aquamarine, blue calcite, turquoise, kyanite, and aqua aura
- Small piece of blue paper and pen (blue ink)
- Jasmine or sandalwood essential oil
- 1 small drawstring bag
- 1 work candle (white, silver, indigo or violet)

Instructions:

Place all of the ingredients on your altar or work space and light the work candle as you say:

"With great joy and faith I greet this Blue Moon."

Anoint the spell candle with the oil, and place it in its holder.

Write the following (or similar) words on the paper: *All good luck is mine.*

Fold the paper in half, and then half again.

Now, say the following (or similar) words and light the spell candle:

"On this rare night shines a rare light,
the magical power of the Blue Moon.
I draw this energy into my life
and all that comes to me will be a boon."

Place one drop of the oil on the paper, then put it in the drawstring bag.

Now pass each crystal, one by one, over the flame of the spell candle (high enough not to burn your fingers!) and place it gently in the bag.

Pull the bag closed and leave it in front of the spell candle until the candle has burned all the way down.

Keep your good luck charm with you on your person, in your car, or in a special place in your home.

At the next Blue Moon, unpack it, bury or burn the paper, and give thanks for all of your good luck!

LUNAR PAPER ECLIPSE SPELL

A Lunar Eclipse is a great time to work both waning and waxing magic in a single spell. In fact, it's very powerful to use both of these approaches on the same magical goal when harnessing Eclipse energy.

For example, if your focus is a health-related goal, you can release illness and attract strength and positive energy. If the intention is prosperity, you can release old limiting patterns or beliefs around money and attract new opportunities or surprise windfalls.

Use construction paper or scrap paper to make your circles. They don't have to be perfect circles, but the paper should be free of any text or images on both sides.

If you're working during a total Lunar Eclipse and want to acknowledge the blood-red color of the Moon at this time, use a dark red candle.

You will need:

- 1 black or dark red candle
- 1 small (3-4 inch) white paper circle
- 1 equally-sized black paper circle
- White and black crayons
- Fire-proof dish

Instructions:

Light the candle.

Write what you want to release on the black circle, using the white crayon.

Write what you intend to attract on the white circle with the black crayon.

Turn the circles over so the blank sides are facing you.

Now, pass the black circle over the white one, in the manner of a total Lunar Eclipse.

Pause briefly when the two circles are exactly aligned and say "*It is done.*"

Then continue the motion until the "paper Eclipse" is complete.

Carefully light the black circle with the candle flame and allow it to burn out in the dish (or in a sink).

You can bury the white circle, make it part of a new magical charm, or add it to a vision board to remind you of what you're bringing into your life with this powerful energy.

MAGICAL OIL BLENDS
FOR LUNAR OCCASIONS

Anoint magical tools and/or wear a few drops of these blends during your spellwork on the New and Full Moons. Using pure essential oils, rather than synthetics, is strongly recommended.

To prevent irritating your skin, be sure to use a carrier oil, such as almond, jojoba, or grapeseed oil, to dilute the essential oils.

Use 2 tablespoons of carrier oil per recipe.

Full Moon Oil Recipe:

- 4 drops jasmine
- 3 drops sandalwood
- 2 drops clary sage

New Moon Oil Recipe:

- 3 drops lemon
- 2 drops rose
- 2 drops sandalwood

*Blended oils will stay good for several months to one year, provided they're stored in a cool, dark place.

FULL MOON RITUAL BATH SALTS

This bath ritual is perfect for a powerful night of Full Moon magic!

You will need:

- 3 tablespoons sea salt
- 1/4 teaspoons dried hibiscus petals
- 1/4 teaspoons dried mugwort leaves
- 1/8 teaspoons anise seed
- 2-3 drops lavender oil

Instructions:

Place the salt in a small bowl.

Place the herbs in a mortar and pestle and gently crush while combining thoroughly.

Pour them into the bowl with the salt and stir again.

Add the oil and stir again.

Add to the bath under running water.

*Note: if your drain clogs easily, use a mesh strainer to catch the herbs when you're finished with your bath.

CHARGING TOOLS
WITH LUNAR ENERGY

Of the many methods for infusing your ritual tools and spell ingredients with magical energy, charging them under the light of the Moon is one of the simplest and most effective.

Moonlight is known to have both cleansing and charging properties, so you don't have to worry about clearing the old energy from your items as a separate step.

For best results, leave your tools out overnight under the Full Moon, or at least in a windowsill where they will receive direct moonlight.

Lunar energy is particularly suited to charging crystals and other mineral stones—particularly those associated with intuitive and psychic abilities. You can really see and feel the effect of the Moon on your crystals the next day—they'll be shiny and new and feel great in your hand!

GARDENING WITH THE MOON

One of the most rewarding ways to tap into the rhythms of lunar energies is through growing your own herbs, vegetables, and flowers.

Whether you've got a sprawling outdoor garden or a few pots on a windowsill, you can work with the phases of the Moon's cycle for optimal success.

Gardening and farming according to lunar phases is rooted in age-old folklore, as our ancestors observed the Moon's effects on their crops.

Of course, we now know that the Moon's gravitational pull on the oceans is also felt in the Earth's subtle bodies of water, which in turn affect the soil. But even if your soil is contained within a garden bed or a pot, the energetic connection you're making to the Moon brings a "green thumb" effect to your efforts!

If you're able, try growing some moon-associated plants, or other magical herbs, to have on hand for an extra boost to your spellwork.

First Quarter (New to waxing Half): This is the best time to plant above-ground crops that produce seeds outside of the fruit, such as grain crops, broccoli and other cruciferous vegetables, spinach and other greens, and most annual herbs.

Second Quarter (waxing Half to Full): Plant above-ground crops that produce their seeds inside the fruit or seed pod, such as beans, tomatoes, peppers, and squash. The two to three days before the Full Moon are the "sweet spot" for planting during this period.

Third Quarter (Full to waning Half): As the waning phase begins, particularly in the first few days after the Full Moon, the time is perfect for planting root vegetables like carrots, potatoes, beets and onions. Bulbs, perennials, and biennials are favored now as well.

Fourth Quarter (waning Half to Dark): This phase is best for weeding, harvesting, pruning, and transplanting crops. Give your houseplants a little extra love at this time as well, and then let everything rest—yourself included!—for a few days before the New Moon.

*Note: if you're working strictly with potted herbs and flowers, or if all of your outdoor plants are of the same type, you can still tend them according to the basic patterns of waxing and waning. Plant, fertilize, and gently weed during the waxing phase, and prune, harvest, and transplant during the waning.

TABLES OF CORRESPONDENCE

Included here are brief tables of correspondence, relevant to anyone looking to work with the Moon's magical energies.

ZODIAC SIGNS
AND MAGICAL PURPOSES

These are the most common magical purposes associated with the Moon as it relates to each sign of the Zodiac.

Of course, to make use of these correspondences you'll need to know which sign the Moon is in at any given time! You can find this information online, or in a Wiccan or other Pagan resource, such as the annual *Witch's Almanac* (see "Suggestions for Further Reading" at the end of this guide).

A good source will also identify when the Moon is void of course, or between signs. Some Witches find that working during void of course periods leads to less effective magic, while others experience no difficulty with spells cast at these times. You may want to experiment with this, and see what works best for you.

Moon in Zodiac Sign	Work Magic Related to...
Aries	new ventures, general health and vitality, self-improvement, difficult conflicts, navigating issues with bureaucracy, leadership, authority, impatience difficult tempers, surgery
Taurus	money, prosperity, real estate, material acquisitions, self-esteem, love, sensuality, gardening and farming, fertility, patience, endurance, commitment, music, the arts, business
Gemini	intelligence, communication, commerce, siblings, writing, teaching, neighbors, dealing with gossip, travel, transportation, public relations, media, networking, adaptability, memory, LGBT issues

Moon in Zodiac Sign	Work Magic Related to...
Cancer	home, family, mothers, children, traditions, weather and climate, security, integrity, water issues (particularly natural bodies of water), psychic abilities, integrity, listening to and assisting others
Leo	love (platonic), self-confidence, self-expression, performing in public, vacation and leisure time, courage, childbirth, taking risks, good cheer, gambling, amusement, creativity, loyalty, fine arts
Virgo	health and healing, diet, business and trade, tools, employment, intelligence and intellect, co-workers, military and police, exercise and fitness, work ethic, debt, cleansing and purification, hunting, pets
Libra	legal matters, justice, marriage, peace, balance, diplomacy, beauty, harmony, team-building, contracts, romance and dating, partnership, art and music, socializing, meeting people, overcoming laziness
Scorpio	regeneration, renewal, sex, death, secrets, divination, psychic development, banishing, willpower, purification, hypnotism, emotional honesty, solitude, courage, transformation, mediumship
Sagittarius	optimism, resilience, generosity, legal matters, education (especially higher education), ethics, dreams, contacting the divine, generosity, fame, publishing, good luck, long journeys, fun, humor, languages

Moon in Zodiac Sign	Work Magic Related to...
Sagittarius	optimism, resilience, generosity, legal matters, education (especially higher education), ethics, dreams, contacting the divine, generosity, fame, publishing, good luck, long journeys, fun, humor, languages
Capricorn	careers, jobs, promotions, fathers, responsibility, solitude, healing from depression, ambition, public recognition, honor, reputation, awards, long term results, government, time management, wisdom
Aquarius	friendship, acquaintances, politics, electronics, freedom, science, extrasensory development, breaking bad habits, problem solving, objectivity, luck, meeting new people, social justice, hope
Pisces	psychic ability, music, spirituality, criminal matters, widows and orphans, reversing bad luck, finding lost items, charity, self-reflection, past lives, facing fears, endings, water (particularly oceans and salt water), dance, drug and alcohol problems

SEASONAL ASSOCIATIONS
AND MAGICAL PURPOSES

These correspondences can be applied in a few different ways.

As discussed in Part Two, each phase of the lunar cycle corresponds to one of the four seasons. So if the Moon is waxing, for example, you can choose a magical purpose for Spring.

Of course, you can also break it down into the eight "seasons," or Sabbats, for more flexibility, and a more evenly aligned distribution around the Wheel of the Year.

If the Moon is at waxing Half, feel free to look to the Summer correspondences in addition to those for Spring.

Finally, you might simply work according to the actual season you're in! This approach is especially effective at the Full Moon.

Moon Phase—Seasonal Association	Work Magic Related to...
Spring	healing, fertility, purification, gardening, environmental concerns, psychic ability, paying debts and bills
Summer	friendship, love, marriage, strength, physical stamina, protection, courage, beauty
Autumn	employment, money, real estate, material acquisitions, transformation, reaping benefits from past efforts
Winter	breaking bad habits, banishment, releasing emotional difficulties, magical study and introspection

SPELL INGREDIENTS
ASSOCIATED WITH THE MOON

These are the most common colors, crystals, flowers, herbs, incense, and oils associated with the Moon. There are more of each, of course, which you can find in your own further explorations!

Colors	Crystals	Flowers
Silver	Moonstone	Hyacinth
White	Pearl	Hibiscus
Royal Blue	Smoky Quartz	Lily
Indigo	Selenite	Lilac
Violet	Quartz Crystal	Iris
Grey	Meteorite	Lotus

Herbs	Incense	Oils
Moonwort	Sandalwood	Lemon Balm
Mugwort	Myrrh	Jasmine
Fennel	Lavender	Sandalwood
Anise Seed	White Sage	Camphor
Evening Primrose	Vervain	Rose
Irish Moss	Jasmine	Clary Sage

RISING AND SETTING TIMES FOR THE MOON

This is a very basic tracking tool for learning to find the Moon in the sky on a daily basis. You can find exact rising and setting times for where you live online. Eventually, as you get into a practice of locating the Moon throughout the course of its cycle, you'll develop an instinctual feel for when to expect—and not to expect—the Moon to appear in your view of the sky.

Moon Phase	Moon Rise	Moon Set
New	Sunrise	Sunset
1st Quarter	Local Noon	Local Midnight
Full	Sunset	Sunrise
3rd Quarter	Local Midnight	Local Noon

CONCLUSION

Hopefully, you are coming away from this guide with a much broader perspective on the Moon than you had before.

Its magical energies, its influence over all life on Earth, and its potential to aid you in manifesting your dreams make this celestial body well worth paying attention to! Of course, as we have seen, you are influenced by the moon whether you pay it any mind or not.

In fact, many Witches and "ordinary folk" alike have remarked that when they keep at least one eye on where the Moon is in its cycle, their lives are less full of roadblocks and unpleasant surprises.

When they forget about the Moon for awhile, life can start to get more chaotic. What many don't realize is that by noticing and acknowledging the Moon, they are attuning to its energies, and therefore living more in harmony with the rhythms of Nature.

Each day provides you with an opportunity to take a moment to connect with the Moon, whether through a formal ritual or a brief, silent greeting. Each phase of the Moon's cycle offers particular energies that you can attune with and harness for your specific magical goals.

This lunar approach to magic offers a richly diverse, yet comfortably cyclical path for you to follow as you continue your never-ending explorations of ritual and spellwork. But whether or not you decide to adopt a structured practice of lunar magic, you will certainly benefit from keeping these rhythms in your consciousness on a regular basis.

If you would like to learn more about Moon magic, be sure to check out some of the sources listed on the following. May the light of the Goddess and the magic of the Moon be with you on your journey!

SUGGESTIONS FOR FURTHER READING

The topic of Moon magic has been written about widely, by Wiccan authors and others who work with the Moon as part of their magical practice.

While you'll no doubt find similar, basic information about the energies and correspondences of the lunar phases in many of these resources, each author has their own individual experiences and perspective on these topics.

As with anything else in Wicca or the larger Pagan world, it's always worth the effort to learn as much as you can in order to deepen your own practice.

This brief list of books offers some solid places to start, as well as a few suggested resources for helping you keep close track of the Moon in your day-to-day life. Happy reading!

Books:

These general sources cover some of the topics from this guide in more detail, as well as plenty of additional Moon lore, from a range of perspectives. For those interested in learning more about the role of astrology in working with the Moon's energies, the last two books are well worth checking out.

Diane Ahlquist, *Moon Spells: How to Use the Phases of the Moon to Get What You Want* (2002)

Zsuzsanna E. Budapest, *Grandmother Moon: Lunar Magic in Our Lives—Spells, Rituals, Goddesses, Legends, and Emotions Under the Moon* (1991)

D.J. Conway, *Moon Magick: Myth & Magic, Crafts & Recipes, Rituals & Spells* (1995)

Dorothy Morrison, *Everyday Moon Magic: Spells & Rituals for Abundant Living* (2003)

Rachel Patterson, *Pagan Portals - Moon Magic* (2014)

Yasmin Boland, *Moonology: Working with the Magic of Lunar Cycles* (2016)

Ann Moura, *Mansions of the Moon for the Green Witch: A Complete Book of Lunar Magic* (2010)

Almanacs and Calendars

In addition to detailed daily information about the Moon's current phase and Zodiac sign, each of these annual publications contains articles on a diverse range of topics of interest to Wiccans and other Witches.

The almanacs in particular are actually worth hanging onto as references long after their calendar information becomes outdated. In fact, you can still find the 2012 Witches' Almanac, which is focused on all things Moon-related, at online retailers.

The datebooks and calendars provide the lunar phase information in a readily-accessible format for easier integration of the cycle into your daily life. These are not the only resources that include these details, however, so feel free to shop around for other possibilities as well!

Llewellyn's Magical Almanac: Practical Magic for Everyday Living (Annual Publication)

The Witches' Almanac (Annual Publication)

The Witches' Almanac: Issue 32—Wisdom of the Moon (Witches' Almanac: Complete Guide to Lunar Harmony) (2012)

Llewellyn's Witches' Datebook (Annual Planner)

Llewellyn's Witches' Calendar (Wall Calendar)

WICCA

WHEEL OF
THE YEAR
MAGIC

*A Beginner's Guide to the Sabbats, with
History, Symbolism, Celebration Ideas,
and Dedicated Sabbat Spells*

LISA CHAMBERLAIN

CONTENTS

INTRODUCTION

If you're reading this guide, you probably already know that Wiccans celebrate several Sabbats, or holidays, over the course of a year. These eight holy days, spaced roughly six weeks apart, make up the Wiccan "Wheel of the Year," a term that emphasizes the ever-turning nature of life on Earth.

Of course, the Wheel of the Year is not unique to Wicca—many other modern Pagan spiritual paths also observe these ancient sacred days, oftentimes with traditions and customs similar to those found within Wicca. The information in this guide is rooted in Wicca, but much of it is applicable to Pagans of all stripes, as well as anyone who is simply curious about the rich traditions surrounding these milestones of the Old Religion.

It's important to note that Wiccans also observe twelve (sometimes thirteen) Esbats, or ritual observances of the Full Moon. These monthly Esbats are often referred to as "the second wheel of the year" and together with the Sabbats make up the full Wiccan religious calendar.

Because a guide of this length could never do justice to each celebration involved in the entire Wiccan year, our focus here will be on the Sabbats, which mark the Sun's journey around the Earth from season to season. This is not intended to dismiss the importance of the Esbats, but simply to allow for a more thorough exploration of the eight "days of power" and what they mean to those who honor them.

In Part One, we'll introduce the general concepts inherent to the Wheel of the Year, a brief history of its development within Gardnerian Wicca, and a framework for approaching the practice of magic as part of your Sabbat celebrations.

Part Two devotes a full chapter to each of the Sabbats: their significance within the context of the ever-changing seasons, the part they play in the mythological cycle of the Goddess and the God, and the spiritual themes they ask us to reflect upon as we celebrate them. You'll also learn about the historical origins of each holiday and the associated traditions and practices that have been handed down over the centuries from our European pagan ancestors.

Finally, you'll find magical correspondences for spellwork and celebration of each Sabbat, as well as spells and other magical workings tailored specifically for each point on the Wheel.

Whether you are just starting out in Wicca, or are a seasoned practitioner looking for new perspectives, may these pages support and inspire your journey.

Blessed Be.

PART ONE

THE WHEEL
AT A GLANCE

INVENTING
THE WHEEL

In the days before clocks and calendars, people marked the passing of time and the turning of the year by following the movements of the Sun and the stars. Their "months" didn't contain 30 or 31 measured days, but instead followed the cycling of the Moon from New to Full and back to New again.

It was Nature that told them what time it was, and our ancestors depended entirely on Nature's clock for their sustenance. A hard winter, a weak harvest or a decline in wild game could mean extreme misfortune and even death. So it's no surprise that they regularly took time to pay homage to Nature, in the form of their gods and goddesses, to express gratitude for their blessings and ask for assistance in the coming season.

The rituals and traditions used to mark the turning of the seasons in the ancient world varied widely across the globe and evolved over time. In the Western world, where Wicca finds its roots, there's a rich diversity of lore from the ancient Egyptians, Greeks, Romans, Celts and Germanic peoples. These cultures worshipped different gods and goddesses and had different names for their holy days, but the dates on which their observations took place were actually fairly consistent.

For example, in early February, the ancient Egyptians celebrated the Feast of Nut in honor of this mother goddess' birthday, while the Romans were busy with the purification and fertility rituals of Lupercalia, a holiday commemorating the mythical founders of Rome. The Celts also saw this as a time of purification as they celebrated Imbolc, and the Swedish Norse observed Disting, a time to honor the feminine spirits of the family. Weather divination was practiced in many cultures on this day, including among Germanic tribes, whose particular custom has survived all the way into the present in the U.S. "holiday" of Groundhog's Day.

Wicca was born out of a desire to reconnect with the spiritual practices of our ancestors—those who lived and worshipped in the old ways, before the Christianization of Europe (and much of the rest of the world). Inspired by the English occult revival of the late 1800s, Gerald Gardner and others set about reviving what they believed was an ancient pan-European religion, nearly wiped out by the Church but still surviving in hidden pockets of England and elsewhere.

An important aspect of the newly-reconstructed "witchcraft," as it was called by Gardner and his coveners, was the observing of the old pagan holidays, or "Sabbats" as they came to be known. These were the feasts and festivals that had long been coopted by the Christian Church in its efforts to stamp out the Old Religion once and for all. In addition to meeting at the Full Moon, Gardner's new 20th-century coven would meet on the occasions of these ancient festivals and enact special rituals to celebrate them.

Originally, Gardner's coven marked only the four cross-quarter days of November 1, February 2, May 1, and August 1. These dates were based on the ancient Celtic calendar, which divided the year into a "dark half," or Winter (from Nov 1st to April 30th) and a "light half," or Summer (from May 1st to October 31st).

In this system, which was based on agricultural cycles, the dates of February 2 and August 1 mark the halfway points, or "cross quarters," of each half of the year. The coven would meet on the evening before the cross-quarter day, which is in line with the Celtic tradition of the new day beginning at sundown. Hence, these Sabbats as envisioned by Gardner were called "November Eve," "February Eve," and so on.

Other pioneers of the new Paganism during this time, such as the Order of Bards, Ovates and Druids, were incorporating additional ancient sacred dates into their practices. For millennia, the Summer and Winter Solstices were of the utmost importance to the Norse and Anglo-Saxon peoples, and many cultures in Mesopotamia and elsewhere observed the Spring and Autumn Equinoxes. Neolithic structures throughout Ireland and the UK suggest that these astronomical occasions were significant to the predecessors of the Celts as well.

Gardner ultimately added these solar holidays to the cross-quarter days, creating what we now know in Wicca as the eight-fold Wheel of the Year. As Wicca evolved and spread, the Sabbat days took on more specific names, usually borrowed from the ancient cultures that celebrated them.

These names vary across traditions, but the most common ones in use today are a blend of Celtic and Norse/Anglo-Saxon names: Yule, Imbolc, Ostara, Beltane, Litha, Lammas, Mabon and Samhain. Aidan Kelly, an influential figure in Wicca and other modern Paganism, is credited with coming up with this naming system in the late 20th century.

Of course, much has been learned since Gardner's day about the original theory of the ancient pan-European religion, or "witch-cult" as it was called—namely that there wasn't one.

It's true that many similarities can be found in ancient practices across wide swaths of Europe, due to the conquest of large territories by the Celts, the Romans, and the Germanic tribes. But each region still had its own distinct religious identity, making for a broad diversity of deities, beliefs, and customs. And there's scant evidence that any one ancient civilization in Europe marked all eight of the modern Sabbats.

Furthermore, the celebrations on these days would not have been only for the "witches" of the time—instead, entire communities participated in rituals and festivities. So people who believe that the Wiccan Wheel of the Year is a historically accurate revival of pre-Christian paganism are essentially incorrect.

Nonetheless, it could be argued that as the Wheel has evolved over the past several decades, via the expansion of Wicca and other modern Pagan belief systems, we now have something that comes closer to a "pan-European witch-cult revival" than Gardner could ever have envisioned. While the ritual component of Sabbat celebrations tends to be specific to Wicca—the honoring of the God and Goddess as viewed through a Wiccan framework—many practitioners also observe traditional customs that date back to antiquity.

For example, the ancient tree-worshipping practice now known as the Maypole is a popular way to celebrate Beltane, while those who work with magical herbs might make a point of gathering some at Litha, when herbs are traditionally thought to be at their most potent.

Indeed, the wide range of practices we see today—whether passed down through the generations or discovered by historians and anthropologists—provides eclectic Wiccans and other Pagans with increasingly more authentic information to choose from as they create their own Sabbat celebrations.

A TIMELESS CYCLE

The ancients lived by a fundamental truth that is often lost in our fast-paced world—that time is circular as much as it is linear.

The Celts understood this intrinsically, as you can see when examining just about any piece of Celtic artwork. The infinite looping of interweaving lines in the knots and crosses evokes a sense of creation without beginning or end. This same "loop" would have been experienced by all who observed the regularly shifting patterns of the Sun's journey across the sky, from its southernmost point at the Winter Solstice to its northernmost point at the Summer Solstice, and back again.

Following the Wheel of the Year helps us integrate this concept of circular time into our lives. As we mark each Sabbat we are consciously witnessing the turning of each season in exquisite detail, honoring the cycles of life and death, of growth and decay. It also helps us to be more often in the present moment, as the steady flow of holidays to prepare for and celebrate keeps us from rushing headlong through the seasons with barely a passing glance at the natural world.

Then there is the sense of rhythm that the Wheel provides—the equal increments of days and weeks between the Sabbats that help us anchor our sense of time passing in a beautiful symmetry. The eight-fold structure gives definition to a truth we've always subconsciously understood—that there are not four seasons but eight, as the "in-between" seasons bridge the gaps between the "cardinal" seasons of winter, spring, summer and autumn.

This cyclical quality is also seen in the dynamic relationship between the Goddess and the God. As the seasons turn, the divine pair shifts from mother and child to co-creative consorts and then back to mother and child.

Each year at the Winter Solstice, the Goddess gives birth to the God, and each spring she is restored to her Maiden aspect as the two grow together. As summer begins they unite as lovers and the God impregnates the Goddess, ensuring that he will be born again after his death in late autumn, when the Mother Goddess once again becomes the Crone.

Indeed, each deity is forever changing aspects—from young to old, from strong to weak and from bountiful to barren. And the non-linear quality of time is even further demonstrated in that both God and Goddess are manifest in more than one aspect at once: the Goddess is both Mother and Crone in the dark, cold months, and both Mother and Maiden in the early spring. The God is a seed in the Goddess' womb even as he ages and dies at the end of the growing season.

We honor these shifting roles and aspects throughout the year, with each Sabbat representing a point in the overarching story. This close participation with the cycles of the season is what some Wiccans refer to as "turning the Wheel."

NAMES AND ORIGINS

The eight Sabbats can be viewed as two interlocking sets of holidays: the cross-quarter days and the solar days.

In many traditions, a further distinction is made between the greater Sabbats and the lesser Sabbats. The cross-quarter days are called the greater Sabbats because they fall at the points where the shifts between seasons are most palpable, and these are considered to be days of strong power. They also happen to be the holidays we have the most detailed information about when it comes to ancient pagan customs, whether it's the Greeks, the Romans, or the Celts.

Many modern Wiccan practices on these days are rooted in what we know about the ancient Irish, who were able to keep much of their early literature safe from destruction during the Dark Ages. This may be why the cross-quarters take their names largely from the Irish traditions: Imbolc (February 2), Beltane (May 1), and Samhain (October 31). The exception here is Lammas (August 1), which is Anglo-Saxon in origin, but many Wiccans and other Pagans use the Irish name Lughnasa for this Sabbat.

Less is known about the specific details of the solstices and equinoxes, but what we do know is mostly rooted in ancient Norse and Anglo-Saxon cultures. The solstices in particular would have been celebrated by those living in the northern reaches of Europe, where the differences in daylight over the course of the year are more stark than elsewhere on the continent.

The names for these solar Sabbats are less historically accurate than the names of the cross-quarter days, with Yule (December 21) being the most traceable back to an actual pagan celebration on that date. The names Ostara (March 21) and Litha (June 21) are related to ancient Norse culture, but were not necessarily the names of holidays observed on those dates. Mabon (Sept 21) is the most "invented" of all the Sabbat names, taken from a Welsh mythological figure loosely related to the mother-son archetype of the Goddess and the God.

Again, these names do vary across Wiccan and other modern Pagan traditions. For example, people on the newly-evolving path of Norse Wicca may use Norse names for all of the Sabbats. Those who align more with the Celts might decline to use the standard names for the solar holidays and simply refer to them as "Summer Solstice," "Autumn Equinox," etc.

However, with all the diversity of names, customs, etc. to be found around the Wheel of the Year, there are usually a few things in common: feasting, ritual, and appreciation for the natural world in all of its beauty and abundance. And for those Wiccans who include spellwork in their practice, the energies surrounding the Sabbats make them excellent opportunities to work magic.

SABBAT MAGIC

Sabbats are known to many Wiccans as "days of power," since they occur at significant moments in the solar year—the solstices and the equinoxes—and at the cross-quarter points in between, when Earth energies are at their height. (Full Moons, or Esbats, are also days of power, but the focus there is on lunar energies.)

Witches often like to include spellwork and/or spellcraft (creating magical oils, incense, amulets, etc.) as part of their Sabbat celebrations. Of course, any type of magic worked with proper focus and intention will have some success no matter what day it is, but since you're already going to spend time at your altar on Sabbat days, you may as well harness the available extra power!

To maximize your magic's potential, it's useful to plan spellwork that aligns with the particular energies of each Sabbat. For example, take advantage of seasonal associations when it comes to choosing a magical goal.

Summer is traditionally a time for workings related to love, marriage, strength and energy, while winter is best suited to banishings, healing work, and magical and spiritual development. Spring is ideal for spellwork involving planting and outward-focused action, while autumn is a time for harvesting and turning our attention to inner work. You can also plan spells that align thematically with each Sabbat—for example, working for romantic goals at Beltane and banishing negative influences at Samhain.

Connecting with our pagan forbears through our actions on Sabbats is another way of strengthening any magical work we may undertake. For the ancients, most of these sacred occasions were fire festivals, honoring the Sun's role in sustaining life.

Bonfires, torches, and associated fire rituals played a central role in the celebrations, and some of these traditions are still practiced to this day. Fire is indeed a potent part of magic, representing light and transformation, and should be part of your Sabbat activities whether or not any spellwork is involved—even if it's in the form of just a few candles on your altar.

Another key component of Sabbat festivities that connects us to our ancestors is the act of preparing and enjoying a feast. The transformation of raw materials (vegetables, grains, animal flesh) into a delicious meal is its own kind of magical co-creation with the Universe. Even if you're celebrating as a solitary Wiccan, you can still incorporate "kitchen witchery" into your Sabbat meal by charging or blessing your food as you prepare it.

Of course, you don't have to work any spells on a Sabbat for the day itself to already be magical. In fact, there are Wiccans who don't practice magic at all, and their Sabbats are no less powerful and life-affirming than anyone else's.

Indeed, many different people from a wide range of Wiccan and other modern Pagan traditions are celebrating on these days, and the cumulative energy of these celebrations—past and present—contributes to the power already inherent in the Earth energies on these occasions.

So know that no matter how you choose to mark the Sabbats, you are participating in an ageless, timeless tradition of honoring Nature and the workings of the Universe, and your contributions are most welcome.

TURNING THE WHEEL

Now that you've been introduced to the origins and development of the Wheel of the Year as a whole, it's time to meet the individual Sabbats that comprise these eight days of power.

In Part Two, we'll take a close look at each of the greater and lesser Sabbats. You'll learn a bit about the historical contexts from which these modern holidays have evolved, and how these sacred days honor the co-creative relationship between the Goddess and the God.

You'll also find tips and ideas for holding your own Sabbat celebrations, and a few suggested spells and other magical workings that correspond with the themes and season of each holiday. So if you keep a Book of Shadows, you might want to grab it now, since you're bound to find information that will help you plan your next Sabbat!

PART TWO

THE SABBATS

OLD TRADITIONS MADE NEW

One of the key qualities of Wicca that has fueled its expansion over the past several decades is its dynamic capacity for reinvention and reinterpretation. There is a basic framework in place in terms of general beliefs and practices, but there's no universally agreed-upon way to go about any of the specifics, including Sabbat celebrations.

There are still lineage-based covens like those in the Gardnerian and Alexandrian traditions, whose members follow ritual protocols established early on in Wicca's development. But even these groups are bound to alter at least some details, as each coven is a unique collection of individuals with their own understanding of the original material. In fact, those familiar with the history of Wicca will recognize that even Gardner revised and reworked his own original Book of Shadows.

And as Wicca has grown and evolved, infinite variations on the older traditions have emerged. This is in large part due to eclectic practitioners, but it's also because creativity and invention are simply part of the experience of the Craft itself. In fact, many people who identify as Wiccans and Witches today feel perfectly comfortable improvising and inventing their rituals and other traditions around the Sabbats.

Therefore, you won't find any instructions about what to do or say during your formal Sabbat rituals in the following pages. (For those who would like help getting started with Wiccan ritual format, examples can be found in many sources in print and online.) Instead, the focus here is on getting a solid sense of what each holiday is all about, so you can begin developing your own approach to celebrating from a well-informed perspective.

In each chapter, we'll explore the seasonal context of the Sabbat and the associated themes that are often incorporated into Wiccan and other Pagan observances, including the stage it represents in the mythological cycle of the Goddess and God. We'll also take a brief tour of what is known of the pagan history behind each Sabbat—the myths, beliefs and customs that have inspired our modern celebrations—and common ways in which these have been incorporated.

PLANNING YOUR SABBAT

Of course, you'll also find suggestions for approaching your own Sabbat celebrations, whether you're a solitary practitioner or working with fellow Witches. Again, the possibilities here are infinite, and your choices will depend on your tradition (or lack thereof), your level of experience, and what each of these days means to you personally. That being said, there are two elements that most Sabbat celebrations have in common: the altar and the feast.

Setting up your altar for a Sabbat is a wonderful way to get into the spirit of the holiday. Whether you have a full-time altar or sacred space, or whether you're sprucing up an end table, it's hardly a Sabbat without special decorations—seasonal symbols, altar cloths, corresponding candles, flowers, herbs and crystals, etc. If you can, start setting up a day or two before the Sabbat, but if this isn't possible you can still start gathering the items you'll put on the altar when the time comes.

The altar is the focal point for your Sabbat ritual, so the more attention you put into it, the more receptive you will be in your connection with the God and Goddess. And it doesn't matter whether your altar is simple or elaborate—it's the energy with which you put it together that matters. You'll find detailed suggestions for altar decorations for each Sabbat under the "Correspondences" heading.

For solitary practitioners, a "feast" may be a little harder to pull off. But this word doesn't have to be taken literally. Whether you cook yourself a nice meal, or simply enjoy a healthy snack, just be sure to treat yourself to some nourishment from Nature at this time. Suggestions for seasonally appropriate foods are also included in the Correspondences in each chapter.

As for magic, you'll find two examples of spellwork in each chapter that are aligned with the seasonal and divine energies of the Sabbat. These can be followed as-is or adapted to suit your individual style. They can also be a springboard for more ideas about how to approach magical work on these days of power.

A NOTE ON DATES

The calendar dates given in this guide are the most commonly observed. However, the actual dates on which these holidays are observed can vary for a few reasons.

When it comes to the solar (or lesser) Sabbats, the exact moment of each solstice and equinox varies from year to year, due to a slight misalignment between the Gregorian calendar and the actual rate of the Earth's rotation around the Sun. For this reason, a range of dates is provided for these holidays.

For cross-quarter (or greater) Sabbats, some sources give the day before, in keeping with the Celtic tradition of the day beginning at sundown, so you will see both options in this guide.

Finally, for those living in the Southern Hemisphere, the dates of the Sabbats are completely reversed, so that Yule falls in June and Litha in December, and so on. These dates are also noted.

Some Wiccans, rather than following the modern calendar, use the movements of the Sun or the Moon to determine their cross-quarter day celebrations. A "cross-quarter" day is technically the astronomical halfway point between the two adjoining solar days—for example, Samhain marks the midpoint between the Autumn Equinox and the Winter Solstice.

The actual midpoint, however, usually occurs closer to November 6 or 7, so some covens and individuals may hold their Samhain celebrations then, instead of October 31st. Others may observe it on the first New Moon of the month, or of the first New Moon of the Zodiac sign in which the cross-quarter day falls.

Obviously, there's a lot of variance here from year to year, so these alternate dates are not cited in the guide, but that doesn't mean you can't follow one of these systems if it resonates with you.

No matter which date you celebrate your Sabbat, just be sure to approach it with joy and reverence for the natural world, the Goddess and God who create and sustain life, and the beauty of the cycle of life and death that keeps the Wheel forever turning.

YULE
(WINTER SOLSTICE)

Northern Hemisphere: December 20-23

Southern Hemisphere: June 20-22

Pronounced: Yool

Themes: rebirth, quiet introspection, new year, hope, setting intentions, celebration of light

Also known as: Winter Solstice, Midwinter, Alban Arthuan, Saturnalia, Yuletide

Celebrated on the date of the Winter Solstice, Yule is the point on the Wheel of the Year when we acknowledge the beginning of the return of the light. The nights have reached their longest point, creating a sense of darkness that is almost overbearing. The air is cold, the deciduous trees are completely bare, and for those in northern climates, the season of snow is in full swing.

Yet as far as the Sun is concerned, this is a turning point toward increased daylight, and the promise that warmth of the growing season will eventually return. The longest night will now be behind us, and the Sun will stay with us later each day, rising ever higher in the sky until the Summer Solstice, the turning point on the opposite side of the Wheel.

However, it will be a few weeks before this is noticeable, as the increase in daylight is only gradual at first. The Sun actually appears to not alter its path across the sky at all during the days around the

Winter Solstice. In fact, the word "solstice" comes from a Latin phrase meaning "sun stands still."

Likewise, much of Nature seems to be still at this point. Birds have migrated south, many animals hibernate, and the snow covering the ground seems to have a quieting effect on the landscape. This is a time of turning inward, hunkering down, and tuning in to our deepest selves.

Many people see these short days and long nights as a time of self-reflection, spiritual study, and intention-setting for the coming year. But before the deep winter sets in, we gather with friends and family to celebrate the renewal of the Sun and the hope that comes with emerging from the darkness. This has always been a traditional time for both spiritual observance and merriment, and still is today, as we can see in the many different holidays and festivities associated with the start of the winter season.

In many Wiccan traditions, Yule is the start of the new year. The seasons of the Wheel, and the annual story of the God and the Goddess have completed the circle and now begin again.

The Goddess gives birth to the God, fulfilling the intention the divine pair set when they coupled at Beltane. As the Sun God, his symbolic death and return to the underworld at Samhain led to the darkness of the past six weeks, and now his rebirth brings back the light. The Goddess has transformed once again from her Crone aspect back to the Mother, who will now rest awhile from her labor and emerge rejuvenated in the spring.

This segment of the mythological cycle is at the heart of the Wiccan understanding of reincarnation—after death comes rebirth into new life. The Sun illustrates this truth through its cyclical disappearance and reappearance. The Earth, which never disappears, represents the never-ending presence of the divine Universe.

WINTER MAGIC AND MERRIMENT

Of all the solar Sabbats, Yule is probably the one most clearly rooted in an ancient pagan holiday, as it takes its name from a festival held in Germanic and Scandinavian cultures around the time of the Solstice (though the original Yule likely lasted for several days).

Of course, many other peoples of the ancient world also observed the Winter Solstice, as we can see by the number of Neolithic monuments—like Newgrange in Ireland—built to align with the sunrise on this day. The Romans celebrated Saturnalia around this time, which involved feasting and exchanging gifts as well as ritual sacrifice. In Persia, this was when worshippers of the god Mithra celebrated his birth. And the Druids of the Celtic Isles are said to have gathered sacred mistletoe and sacrificed cattle on the solstice.

But while some forms of Wicca may base their Yule celebrations on some of these other regional traditions, in general the Norse and Anglo-Saxon customs that give the Sabbat its name are what the day is best known for.

In the lands of Northern Europe, the Solstice festivities were the last opportunity for most people to socialize before the deep winter snows kept them from being able to travel. Great gatherings were held by the Germanic tribes where feasting, drinking, and ritual sacrifice of livestock took place. Bonfires were lit and toasts were drunk to the Norse gods such as Odin and Thor.

These activities helped ensure a prosperous growing season in the coming new year, which was dawning now with the Sun's reemergence from the dark shadows. Some of the traditions observed during these ancient festivals—such as the Yule log, decorating with evergreen boughs and branches, warm alcoholic beverages known as wassail, and group singing—continued on through the centuries and are still part of many Christmas celebrations today.

The Yule log in particular was widespread in Europe, with many different regional customs attached to it. Traditionally made from a large log of oak, it was decorated with pine boughs, holly, or other evergreen branches and doused with cider or ale before being lit at the start of the festivities. In many places, this fire was lit with a piece of wood saved from the previous year's Yule log.

The log was supposed to be harvested from the land of the household, or else given as a gift—to purchase it was deemed unlucky. The Yule fire was tended so that it didn't burn out on its own, in part so that a piece of the log could be saved to start the following year's fire.

The length of time for the fire to burn varied but was usually between 12 hours and 12 days.

The Yule festivities—caroling, games, the exchanging of gifts—took place around the warmth of the fire. In some places, the ashes from the Yule fire were used to make magical charms, sprinkled over the fields to encourage the crops, or tossed into wells to purify the water. As with so many other pagan festivals, we can see that the magical power of fire was alive and well at Yule!

The most obviously pagan remnant surviving in today's holiday traditions is probably the use of mistletoe. This parasitic plant (called so because it grows attached to a host plant, usually oak or apple trees) was significant to both the Norse and Celtic cultures, as well as the ancient Greeks and Romans. It's not clear why "kissing under the mistletoe" became a tradition, but it's thought to come from an ancient Norse myth involving the goddess Frigga and the death and restoration of her son Baldur.

The significance of mistletoe at the Winter Solstice likely comes from the Druids, who viewed the plant's ability to stay green while the oak it grew on was without leaves as a sign of its sacred powers. The mistletoe was ritually harvested at this time with a golden sickle and fed to the animals to ensure fertility. It was also valued for its protective properties, particularly against fire and lightning, and was used in medieval times for healing.

Interestingly, once the Christian Church had coopted Yule and other Solstice festivals in its quest for domination, mistletoe was prohibited as a decoration, most likely due to its association with magic.

CELEBRATING YULE

Many covens meet just before dawn on the day of the Solstice to hold their Yule rituals, and then watch the rebirth of the God enacted as the Sun rises. In some traditions, the fires and/or candles are lit in encouragement of the Sun God's emergence, welcoming his returning light. Themes of ritual may include regeneration, light in the darkness, and setting intentions for the new year.

In some Wiccan traditions, this is the time to ritually reenact the battle between the Oak King and the Holly King. These twin brothers represent the opposing poles of the Sun's annual journey through the seasons. The Holly King, representing the dark half of the year, reigns until the Winter Solstice, when he is cut down by the Oak King, who heralds in the beginning of the waxing daylight. This cyclical story serves as a reminder that light and dark are both essential parts of existence in Nature—neither can exist without the other.

For solitary Wiccans who live "double lives" as far as mainstream society is concerned, Yule can be a challenging Sabbat to make time for, swamped as so many are with the obligations of the Christmas season. However, since plenty of the traditions associated with both holidays overlap, it's easy enough to infuse more conventional practices with a little Yule magic.

For example, hang a sprig of holly above your door to ensure protection and good fortune for your family and your guests. Magically charge your Christmas tree ornaments before placing them on the branches. Whisper an incantation to the Goddess over any cookies, spiced cider, or any other holiday goods you make for your friends, family or coworkers. You can spread the blessings of your own personal holiday throughout your community without anyone even knowing it!

For those without indoor hearths, a Yule log can be fashioned from a small tree branch—flatten it on one side so it will sit evenly on the altar and drill small holes to place candles into. Go outside and gather boughs of fir, juniper or cedar, as well as pinecones, holly berries, and any other "natural decor" to bring the energies of protection, prosperity, and renewal into your home.

Use mistletoe to bring peace and healing to your life by placing leaves in a sachet or hanging it over your door. Honor the rebirth of the Sun by inscribing discs, pinwheels, or other solar symbols into a large red, orange or yellow pillar candle. Light it at dawn on the day of the Winter Solstice to welcome the Sun and the new beginning of the Wheel of the Year.

YULE CORRESPONDENCES

<u>Colors:</u> red, green, gold, silver, white, orange

<u>Stones:</u> bloodstone, garnet, emerald, diamond, ruby, clear quartz

<u>Herbs:</u> bayberry, blessed thistle, frankincense, chamomile, mistletoe, ivy, rosemary, all evergreens, oak and holly trees

<u>Flowers:</u> sunflowers, dried flowers from summer

<u>Incense:</u> frankincense, cedar, juniper, pine, cinnamon, myrrh, bayberry

<u>Altar decorations/symbols:</u> candles, evergreen wreaths and boughs, holly, mistletoe, pinecones, Yule log, snowflakes, pinwheels, yellow discs, other solar symbols and imagery

<u>Foods:</u> fruits, nuts, baked goods, cider, spiced cider, eggnog, ginger tea, wassail

INNER LIGHT MEDITATION

No matter which holiday(s) you observe in December, it's hard to avoid the noise and bustle of the general holiday season. The commercialism of mainstream society is at its height, there are many social gatherings to go to, and everything seems to feel busier.

It can be a struggle to stay balanced and grounded at this time, especially for people who are strongly affected by the lack of sunlight at this point in the year. This simple visualization can help you connect with your inner light, your center, where your connection to the divine resides.

Meditation is very helpful for people from all walks of life. For Witches, it's a key tool for cultivating a magical state of mind. Here, the candle is a physical symbol for what you're connecting to on the ethereal plane: your inner flame. Adding a little greenery to the scene, even if it's just a few pine needles, brings in the Earth element as well, but it's not strictly necessary for the meditation.

You will need:

- 1 white votive candle
- Small evergreen (pine, cedar, etc.) branch or bough (optional)

Instructions:

Arrange the evergreen on your altar in a visually pleasing manner.

Light the candle and sit quietly, gazing at the flame for a few moments. Then gently close your eyes.

See the flame as a white light spreading from the center of your heart throughout the rest of your body. Hold this visualization and breathe deeply and slowly.

When you find you've wandered off in your mind, gently return your focus to the white light suffusing your entire being.

After 5 to 10 minutes, allow the light to relax back into the form of a candle flame sitting in the center of your heart. When you feel ready, open your eyes. All is well.

MAGICAL YULE BREW

This delicious tea is a nice non-alcoholic alternative to the traditional wassail, though you can turn it into a hot toddy if you like by adding whiskey, brandy or vodka.

Wassail (mulled cider or wine) was originally part of fertility magic among the ancient Norse. It was poured onto the ground at Midwinter to encourage abundant crops in the coming year.

To turn this tea into a magical brew, be sure to charge all ingredients before making it, and say a blessing as you pour the water over the tea and herb mixture. Then drink it in advance of (or during) ritual and/or spellwork.

This recipe is for one cup, but you can adapt it to serve more. Just add one teabag, one lemon slice and one cinnamon stick for each additional person and increase the rest of the ingredients as you see fit.

If you don't have muslin bag or cheesecloth to keep the herbs and spices in while steeping, you can let them float loose in the pot and use a strainer when pouring the tea into mugs. If you don't have a teapot, use a large mug or bowl and cover it with a plate while the tea is steeping.

You will need:

- 1 cup hot (boiled) water
- 1 teabag of black tea
- 1 lemon slice
- 5 whole cloves
- ½ teaspoon dried chamomile
- ¼ teaspoon allspice berries
- Pinch grated ginger
- 1/8 teaspoon orange zest
- 1 cinnamon stick
- Honey to taste
- Muslin bag or square piece of cheesecloth and kitchen twine (optional)
- Teapot

- Mug(s)

Instructions:

Place the herbs and spices except for the lemon, cloves, and cinnamon stick into a muslin bag or cheesecloth sachet.

Place this into the teapot along with the teabag.

Pour the hot water over the tea and herbs and cover, letting steep for 3-5 minutes.

Stud the lemon slice with the cloves.

Pour the steeped tea into the mug and add the lemon slice.

Sweeten with honey and stir with the cinnamon stick. Enjoy!

IMBOLC

Northern Hemisphere: February 1st or 2nd

Southern Hemisphere: August 1st or 2nd

Pronounced: IM-bulk, IM-molg, or imb-OLC

Themes: quickening, hope, renewal, fertility, purification, hearth & home, return of the light

Also known as: Brigid's Day, Oimelc, Feast of Torches, Feast of Pan, Lupercalia, Snowdrop Festival, Feast of the Waxing Light

Although the Spring Equinox is our modern designation for the official beginning of spring, it was Imbolc that traditionally heralded the end of winter in the pagan world.

As the mid-point of the traditional dark half of the year, which begins with Samhain and ends at Beltane, Imbolc marks the time when the grip of winter begins to soften and the Earth starts to come back to life. For people who live in northern climates, where snow and ice dominate the landscape, this is truly a celebration of hope and possibility, as the light grows stronger each day, and subtle signs of the coming of spring begin to emerge.

The days are noticeably lengthening now, as the Sun God's power begins to grow. Among different Wiccan traditions he is described variously as an infant nursing at the Goddess' breast and as a young boy making his way toward maturity. Either way, he is a waxing presence in the sky, higher and more visible with each passing day.

The Goddess, in the form of the Earth, is stirring from her rest following the birth of the God. We see this manifesting as the frozen ground begins to thaw, crocuses and daffodils poke through the surface, and the first birds pass through on their return migration from the southern climates. This is the time when the three-fold aspect of the Goddess shifts from Crone back into Maiden, as the air takes on a hint of youthful energy in the anticipation of warmer days just around the corner.

Our ancestors paid close attention to these early signs of spring. In fact, in the earliest days, the actual date of festival would have been determined by them—for example, once the blackthorns came into bloom.

The cross-quarter day was a time for weather divination in many cultures. In Celtic lore, the length of the winter was determined by the divine hag Cailleach, who would come out to gather the last of her firewood. If she wanted to make the winter last awhile longer, she would make bright, sunny weather on Imbolc—this way she would enjoy a long day of gathering plenty of wood. If she slept through the day, the weather would be gloomy and cold, and the people would know that winter was nearly over.

A Scottish tradition held that Brighid's serpent emerged from under the Earth on Imbolc to test the weather. If it remained above ground, the winter would end soon, but if it returned to its home, another month or more of cold weather was in store. Germanic tribes followed a similar custom with bears and badgers, which in later centuries was adapted to the groundhog and his shadow on Groundhog's Day in the U.S.

Imbolc also marks the beginning of the agricultural season, as the soil is being readied for the first planting and herd animals prepare to give birth. Farmers make needed repairs to their equipment before the season starts in earnest, and rituals for blessing tools and seeds are held at this time—a tradition going back for centuries, if not longer. In every aspect of life—for humans, animals and plants—it's time to start moving around again after the long winter's rest.

The name "Imbolc" itself comes from the ancient Irish and has been translated as "in the belly," referring to the pregnancy of ewes. A related name for the holiday is "Oimelc," meaning "ewe's milk," though this name seems more in use by modern Pagans than it was by the ancient Celts. These milk-producing livestock were crucial for survival for rural people in pre-modern times, especially at this point in the winter, when food stores might be running low or completely empty. So the onset of lambing season was definitely an occasion for celebration!

Purification is another central focus at Imbolc, stemming from the oldest days when dwellings had to be shut tight against the cold for months and bathing was a very infrequent activity. At the first sign of thaw, it was time to throw open the doors, cleanse the house of the stuffy, stale air, and jump into the nearest body of water (once the ice had thawed, of course!). Sunlight was also a purifying force—a manifestation of the Element of Fire—and was taken advantage of as much as possible for renewing the body and the spirit.

BRIGHID, GODDESS OF FIRE

Although each of the cross-quarter days has Celtic roots, Imbolc may be the most Celtic-influenced of the Wiccan Sabbats. While it's true that some forms of Wicca take their inspiration for this holiday from other peoples of pre-Christian Europe, such as the Greeks or the Norse, the most widely used name for is still Imbolc (or "Imbolg," in some areas).

The celebration of Imbolc in Ireland, Scotland and the Isle of Man goes back into pre-written history, and this feast is mentioned in some of the earliest surviving Irish literature. The significance of the cross-quarter day may even predate the Celts themselves, in fact—some of the neolithic monuments in Ireland are actually aligned so that the Sun lights up their inner chambers on this day.

Many Wiccans borrow more than just the name of the Sabbat from the Celts—they also honor the goddess Brighid, who was traditionally the central focus of Imbolc celebrations in Celtic lands. Like the Wiccan goddess, Brighid is three-fold, or "triune" goddess, with aspects that align with the Maiden, Mother and Crone archetypes. In Irish mythology, she rules the three areas of smithcraft, healing and poetry, all of which were powerful activities in Celtic culture.

As a healer, Brighid is associated with many springs and holy wells that were known for their healing, purifying properties. Her cauldron of inspiration sustained poets and bards, and her co-creative powers extended to midwifery and crafting.

Her rule over smithcraft, or metalworking—the alchemical art of transforming raw materials into weaponry and tools—is part of her association with the Element of Fire. In addition, she is said to have been born at sunrise, with a tower of flame bursting from her head and reaching all the way to heaven. She is called "keeper of the sacred flame," and in pre-Christian times her priestesses kept a perpetual fire in her honor at a temple in Kildare, Ireland.

Brighid is also considered the guardian of home and hearth, and was invoked to protect the herds and assist in providing a fruitful harvest. She was associated with the cow, a symbol of motherhood and life sustenance, as well as with the light half of the year, so her presence at this time in late winter was very important to the people.

On Imbolc Eve, Brighid was said to visit the households of those who invited her, and bestow blessings on the inhabitants. Various customs for inviting her were practiced throughout the lands where she was worshipped.

The most common included making her a bed out of a basket with white bedding, and making a straw doll-like figure of Brighid (called a Brídeóg). These corn dollies, as they are also called, were carried from door to door so each household could offer a gift to the goddess.

Families would have a special meal and save some of the food and drink to leave outside for Brighid, along with clothing or strips of cloth for her to bless. The following morning, the family would inspect the ashes of their smoored fire for any marks that showed Brighid had indeed entered the house. The cloth would be brought back inside, now imbued with healing and protective powers.

"Brighid's crosses" were also made from stalks of wheat, formed into a square, an equilateral cross, or an ancient protection symbol resembling a counter-clockwise swastika that was found in various cultures throughout the ancient world. These were hung over the entrances of homes and stables to protect the household from fire, lightning, and any threat to the animals and the harvest. The crosses would be left hanging throughout the year, until the following Imbolc, and are still used in some places today.

Brighid was such a central part of Irish pagan culture that the Christian Church eventually turned her into a saint as part of their religious conquest, and Imbolc is known throughout Ireland as "Brighid's Day." The cross-quarter day was further coopted across Europe by the invention of Candlemas, a Christian holy day that involved the making and blessing of candles for the coming year. Many Wiccans and other Pagans with less specifically-Celtic leanings also use the name Candlemas for this Sabbat.

CELEBRATING IMBOLC

Fire plays a big role in most Wiccan Imbolc traditions. At coven celebrations, a high priestess may wear a crown of lit candles or carry tapers during ritual. This is done in honor of the Goddess stepping into her Maiden aspect and the God's growth into boyhood.

Candles are lit in each room of the house to welcome the Sun. Bonfires are held if the weather is fair, and any evergreen decorations from the Yule Sabbat are burned as a way of letting go of the past season, or even the past year.

For Wiccans, Brighid's status as a Fire goddess makes her an appropriate deity to be recognized on this Sabbat that celebrates the return of the Sun. You can honor her in a variety of ways—by visiting a natural spring or holy well and making offerings, cleaning and purifying your home, lighting candles for her at your altar, or even engaging in writing or other creative activities.

Try making a Brídeóg to place on your altar, and make a Brighid's bed for her to rest in. If you made a "Corn Mother" for Lammas last year, you can repurpose it, dressing her this time in white, yellow or pink (think "Maiden" colors). The bed can be a small basket, a wooden box, or even a well-decorated shoe box. Just be sure to make it comfortable and attractive, with blankets and flowers, ribbons, etc.

Place your Brídeóg in the bed near your hearth (or altar, if you don't have a fireplace). Some traditions leave a small wand with her, which she can use to bless your home. You can also make your own Brighid's cross to hang over your doorway. Instructions for these Imbolc crafts can be easily found online or in other print sources.

Other traditional Imbolc activities include going for walks or hikes to look for signs of spring in the surrounding countryside, taking a ritual bath for physical and energetic purification, and decorating and blessing farm equipment (such as ploughs) for the coming season. Placing a besom, or ritual broom, by the front door symbolizes sweeping out the stale energy of winter and allowing fresh new energy to enter your home and your life.

As with all cross-quarter Sabbats, a special feast is a great idea, particularly on Feb 1st, or "Imbolc Eve." Bringing food to those in need after the long winter—such as homeless shelters and elderly shut-ins—is an excellent way to raise abundance energy for your community.

Finally, Imbolc is a good time to perform self-dedication rituals, or to undergo coven initiation if you are in a position to do so.

IMBOLC CORRESPONDENCES

<u>Colors:</u> red, white, yellow, pink

<u>Stones:</u> garnet, ruby, onyx, bloodstone, amethyst

<u>Herbs:</u> angelica, basil, bay leaf, myrrh, coltsfoot, heather

<u>Flowers:</u> snowdrops, violets, crocus, daffodils, forsythia

<u>Incense:</u> myrrh, cinnamon, violet, wisteria, jasmine, vanilla

<u>Altar decorations/symbols:</u> white flowers, potted bulbs, Brighid's cross, Brídeóg, sheep, cows, ploughs, cauldron, poems or poetry book, candles or candle wheel

<u>Foods:</u> pumpkin and sunflower seeds, poppyseed pastries, dairy products, early spring vegetables

HEARTH AND HOME
PURIFICATION RITUAL

You don't have to be a Witch to notice that the energy and mood of a home is always improved by a thorough cleaning. But making a magical experience out of it takes it to a whole new level!

If you need to do this cleaning in stages, start a couple of days ahead of time. Then put the finishing touches on your cleaning job right before the ritual.

You will need:

- Bowl of water
- Rosemary essential oil or fresh / dried rosemary
- 1 blue candle
- Smudge stick of sage and lavender or sweetgrass

Instructions:

First, clean your house from top to bottom.

This includes the kitchen, which is the modern-day "hearth" for people who don't have working fireplaces in their homes. Clear away any cobwebs lurking in neglected corners, dust and wipe down all surfaces, sweep, mop, vacuum, etc. For best results, use all-natural cleaning agents made with essential oils, rather than chemical products.

Be sure to give extra attention to any ritual/magical objects such as your altar, tools, crystals, etc. If you've been hanging onto any charms or other magical crafts that seem to have finished serving their purpose, now is a good time to respectfully dispose of them.

If weather permits, keep a window open or a door cracked while you clean, and be sure to listen to music that puts you in a happy mood.

When the house is ready, light the candle. Add 3 drops of rosemary to the water and say the following (or similar) words:

*"I give thanks to the purifying essence of Fire.
I give thanks to the purifying essence of Water.
I call on them to bless and protect this home.
So let it be."*

Place the blessed water in front of the candle.

Light the smudge bundle and carry it through each room in the house.

Walk in a clockwise motion, wafting the smoke into every corner.

Open the doors and windows as much as possible, and be sure to keep the front door open for at least a few minutes after the smudging. (This allows any unwanted energy to exit your home.)

Finally, sprinkle a few drops of the rosemary water over the windowsills and doorways in each room.

The candle can be left to burn out on its own, or snuffed and lit again later for ordinary uses.

IMBOLC SEED AND CANDLE SPELL

This spell draws on the symbolic power of seeds at the center of the "hearth" created by three candles. The candles represent the three-fold realms of Brighid, but calling on her directly for assistance isn't required. (But if you feel a connection with her, then by all means ask!) Use this spell to set the tone for the coming growing season in the realms of creativity, healing and abundance.

To prepare, spend some time identifying your goals. You might have three separate goals, such as finding new ideas and energy for a creative project; addressing a physical or emotional injury; and securing a new home. Or, you may have one goal that can be related to each of these domains in some way. You may want to do some journaling and/or meditating to help you clarify what you want to manifest at this time.

If possible, take a ritual bath before working this spell. As always, feel free to tailor the words to suit your own style and beliefs.

You will need:

- 1 yellow Goddess candle
- 1 red God candle
- 3 white spell candles or tea lights
- Small handful (or seed packet) of basil, pumpkin or sunflower seeds
- Small ceramic, stone, glass or wooden bowl

Instructions:

Set up your altar with Imbolc-themed items and imagery.

When you're ready to start, light the Goddess candle and say "*I welcome and give thanks to the awakening Earth.*"

Light the God candle and say "*I welcome and give thanks to the strengthening Sun.*"

Place the seeds into the bowl (if they're in a packet, pour them out).

Hold the bowl in your hands for a moment. Visualize sending your personal power into each seed. See the bowl filling with light in your mind's eye.

Raise the bowl toward the sky and charge the seeds with your voice by saying "*Through these seeds of the Earth will come many blessings.*"

Now place the bowl on the altar and arrange the three white candles around it in a triangle shape. The candle at the top of the triangle represents inspiration. The bottom right candle is for healing, and the bottom left for abundance.

Light the top candle and say: "*By the power of the word I am inspired to right action.*"

Light the right-hand candle and say: "*By the healing waters of the well I am purified.*"

Light the left-hand candle and say: "*By the fire of the forge I create my abundance.*"

Now spend a few moments gazing upon your work. Give thanks again to the Goddess and the God. If you like, seal your spell with the words "*It is done*" or "*Blessed Be.*"

Leave the bowl in place until the candles have burned all the way down.

Save the seeds for planting when it's appropriate to do so. You can also include them in any kind of abundance charm/sachet or else scatter them over the Earth outside of your home.

OSTARA
(SPRING EQUINOX)

Northern Hemisphere: March 19-21

Southern Hemisphere: September 20-23

Pronounced: OH-star-ah

Themes: balance, renewal, action, beginnings, hope, new possibilities

Also known as: Alban Eiler, Rites of Spring, Eostra's Day, Vernal Equinox, March Equinox, Spring Equinox, Lady Day, Bacchanalia

As the first solar Sabbat of the calendar year, Ostara marks the Spring Equinox, one of two points in the Sun's journey at which day and night are of equal length.

The Sun has crossed the "celestial equator," and will shine on Earth for longer each day until it reaches its zenith at the Summer Solstice. For Earth's inhabitants, this is a fortuitous moment, as the scarcity of winter comes to an end and the growing season begins in earnest. On the modern calendar, this is the first day of spring.

Depending on where you live, there may still be snow on the ground, but the Earth is beginning to thaw and rivers rise and overflow their banks. Green grass and spring flowers emerge, lambs, rabbits and chicks are born, and the promise of further new life is felt on the breeze, which is milder than it was just a few weeks ago.

The waxing light is truly felt now, as the Sun's power seems to quicken. The lengthening of the days, first perceived at Imbolc, seem to be growing at an even faster rate as the Sun sets later and further north with each passing day. But just at this moment, the light and the dark exist in equal measure, and this gives Ostara its primary theme of balance.

This balance is observed not only between night and day, but also generally in weather patterns—the harsh, bitter cold of winter is behind us and the relentless heat of summer has yet to arrive. In colder climates, it's not unusual for spring and winter to take turns during these days, with one day feeling more like February and the next more like May. Nonetheless, the fertility of the Earth becomes more and more undeniable as the slow energies of winter give way to the fresh new vibrancy of spring.

This is a time to reunite with the Earth in a tactile way after many months spent largely indoors. Gardening begins in earnest now, as soil is prepared and seed trays are set out in the sunlight to sprout. Those who practice green Witchcraft may perform seed-blessing rituals if they did not already do so at Imbolc.

Magical gardens are plotted out in order to grow the herbs, flowers and vegetables that will later be harvested for feasting, ritual and spellwork. As the first green shoots poke up through the soil, we truly begin the active half of the Wheel of the Year, turning our focus to outward action until the inward, passive half begins again at the Autumn Equinox.

Ostara is also a time to reflect on the balance between the male and female energies of the Universe, each of which requires the other to exist. This gender polarity is at the heart of traditional Wicca, with the Goddess and the God in constant co-creation throughout the changing of the seasons. At this point on the Wheel, the Goddess of the Earth is in her fertile Maiden aspect, while the Sun God grows into his maturity. There is a youthful joy between the two as they make their forays into romance and desire.

In some Wiccan traditions, this is considered the time when the divine pair comes together to conceive the next incarnation of the God, who will be born nine months later at Yule. In many others, the coupling of the divine pair happens at Beltane, when the new energies of growth and light have progressed further into wild abundance.

Nonetheless, in Nature we see the mating of animals and insects is well underway as "spring fever" takes hold.

FERTILITY AND THE GODDESS OF THE DAWN

As midpoints of the solar year, the equinoxes were not typically as widely celebrated as the solstices in pagan Europe. However, there are megalithic sites in Great Britain that align with the Sun on this day, as there are in many other parts of the world.

Many ancient cultures in the Mediterranean region did hold festivals during this time, such as Sham el-Nessim, an Egyptian holiday which celebrates the beginning of spring and can be traced back almost 5,000 years. In Persia, the festival of Nowruz, (meaning "new day") marked the Spring Equinox, and the Jewish calendar sets the dates for Passover based on where the New Moon falls in relation to this day.

In northern Europe, the Latvian festival of Lieldienas was a pre-Christian equinox holiday before it was absorbed into the Christian Easter. And the Norse pagans are said to have honored their female deities with a festival called Dísablót, though some sources place this holiday at the Autumn Equinox or closer to Imbolc.

The Scandinavian tribes and the Anglo-Saxons are where most of our modern Ostara traditions come from, most particularly in the name of this Sabbat. A Saxon goddess named Eostre (also spelled Eostra) is described by an 8th-century scholar who mentions a feast held in her honor at springtime. Little is known about her, and even less is known about her Germanic equivalent, Ostara, for whom the month of April was named in ancient Germanic languages.

However, many place names in some Scandinavian countries suggest that this goddess was fairly widely worshipped before the Christianization of Europe. The name "Eostre" has been translated as "east," "dawn," and "morning light," and so she has seemed a fitting deity to honor at the beginning of the growing season, even if much of the symbolism and lore about her in modern Wicca and other forms of

Paganism has essentially been borrowed from other, better-known goddesses like the Norse Freya.

Symbols and customs of Ostara are recognizable to many as being part of the "Easter" season, such as the rabbit or hare and the egg—both symbols of fertility. The hare—a larger, more rural relative of the rabbit—is believed to be an ancient symbol of the Earth goddess archetype. Hares were also associated with the Moon, and in some places with witches, who were thought to be able to transform themselves into these quick-moving animals.

The fertility association is fairly obvious, as rabbits are known for their fast and prolific reproductive abilities. But there is also an element of honoring the Sun through hare symbolism, as these animals are usually nocturnal, but come out into the daylight during Spring to find their mates. Rabbits and eggs have traditionally gone together, both in ancient days and in modern Easter customs. This stems from our pagan ancestors' observations that plover eggs could sometimes be found in abandoned hares' "nests" in the wild.

The egg itself was a potent symbol of new beginnings and the promise of coming manifestations in many cultures. Painted eggs were part of the ancient Persian Nowruz celebrations, and egg hunts have been traced back at least 2,000 years to Indian and Asian spring customs.

In Anglo-Saxon England, eggs were buried in gardens and under barns as a form of fertility and abundance magic. Offerings of eggs were made to female deities in ancient Scandinavia and in Germany. Interestingly, the egg also speaks to the theme of balance at Ostara, through the tradition of standing an egg on its end in the moments right around the exact time of the Equinox.

Of all the Sabbats, Ostara is the most clear example of how the Christian Church went about converting the pagan populations of northern Europe. By choosing the spring for its own celebration of renewal (in the form of the resurrection of Jesus) and adopting the name of this older festival, it effectively absorbed and dissolved this and other Spring Equinox holidays. However, as with Yule and Samhain, the old pagan customs and traditions have stubbornly stuck around, and are even widely practiced in mainstream society.

CELEBRATING OSTARA

As the weather grows warmer, Ostara is a particularly wonderful time to get outdoors and take in the seasonal changes taking place all around you. If you haven't been in the habit of truly noticing spring's unfolding before, choose a place to visit regularly and study the transformation of the trees and other plant life.

Greet the bees and other insects with joy as they begin to appear, and thank them for their role in sustaining life. Take every opportunity you can to watch the Sun set just a little later each evening. And if you don't already have a garden to prepare, consider starting one—even if you only have a windowsill to grow a magical herb or two.

Coven rituals often focus on the goddess Ostara or another goddess of spring. Witches may meet just before dawn to watch the Sun rise on this perfectly balanced day. Dyeing eggs is a fun activity to do with fellow Wiccans, perhaps using color correspondences to create magical eggs for later spellwork.

Natural objects are always a welcome part of rituals at any time of the year, but especially at the Spring Equinox, the first Sabbat after winter when flowers, buds and blossoms are truly available to be gathered. Sprinkle petals around your altar, float them on water in your cauldron, and wear them in your hair if you like, but be careful to harvest spring wildflowers responsibly, as they serve as much-needed food sources for our much-needed pollinators!

OSTARA CORRESPONDENCES

<u>Colors:</u> yellow, light green, light pink, blue, all pastel shades

<u>Stones:</u> amethyst, aquamarine, jasper, moonstone, rose quartz

<u>Herbs:</u> Irish moss, lemongrass, meadowsweet, catnip, spearmint, cleavers, dogwood and ash trees, woodruff

<u>Flowers:</u> daffodils, honeysuckle, iris, violets, Easter lilies, roses, dandelions, tulips, lilacs

Incense: jasmine, rose, violet, lotus, magnolia, ginger, sage, strawberry, lemon

Altar decorations/symbols: spring flowers, seeds, potted plants, colored eggs, rabbits/hares, birds, pinwheels, yellow discs, other solar symbols and imagery, ladybugs, bumblebees

Foods: eggs, honey, sprouts, dandelion greens, strawberries, all spring vegetables, pumpkin and sunflower seeds, pine nuts

BARK AND FLOWER
BALANCING SPELL

Both the Spring and the Fall Equinoxes provide excellent opportunities to work for balance in our lives. This can mean achieving better physical health, learning how to deal more skillfully with an emotional challenge, or balancing the monthly budget.

Anything you're dealing with that's hindering your ability to make progress in the outer world is a good area to focus on releasing, so that the energies of positive manifestation have more room to come into your life. For best results, identify a goal that aligns with the physical, mental or emotional realm in order to take full advantage of the magical correspondences of your chosen spring flower.

As for the bark, this should be gleaned (i.e. gathered from the ground) and *not* cut from a living tree. Many trees actively shed their bark at the onset of spring in order to make room for their own new growth.

Trees associated with establishing balance include ash, birch, cedarwood, poplar, willow and white oak. If none of these grow where you live, look up the magical correspondences of the trees that do grow in your area, or ask the God and Goddess to guide you in finding the right bark for this spell.

Flowers used in balancing magic include:

Mental: daffodil, iris, lilac, violet (yellow candle)
Emotional: crocus, daffodil, iris, violet, tulip (pink or light blue candle)
Physical: alpine aster, iris, honeysuckle, lilac (green/light green candle)

You will need:

- Piece of gleaned bark
- Handful of flower petals
- Spell candle in a color corresponding to your goal
- Pencil (or ink and quill)

Instructions:

Start by meditating on your goal.

What does *balance* in this situation or area of your life look and feel like to you? Identify a word or short phrase that encapsulates the achievement of your goal, such as "optimal health," "harmony in the home" or "all bills paid."

Write this on the bark. Don't worry if the pencil lead doesn't show up, as the letters are still being traced into the essence of the bark's energy.

Light the candle and lay the bark on your altar or work space.

Sprinkle the daffodils around the bark in a circle three times, moving clockwise.

With each rotation, say the following (or similar) words:

> *"As the day is balanced with the night,*
> *and the darkness balanced with the light,*
> *I find balance in my life."*

Allow the candle to burn out on its own.

Within 24 hours, return the bark to the Earth, either where you found it or another place in Nature.

OSTARA EGG
GARDEN FERTILITY SPELL

Many cultures around the world have long traditions of using eggs in magic, for healing, divination, protection and other purposes. Here, the properties of fertility and promise inherent to the egg is combined with the same energies that are so magnified at the height of Spring.

For those already preparing their gardens, this is a highly opportune time to work this spell, as you're already out digging in the soil! But if you don't have a garden, shift the focus to creating an abundant and thriving home, and bury the egg in your yard.

<u>You will need:</u>

- 1 hard-boiled egg
- Green marker or green paint and brush

<u>Instructions:</u>

Boil the egg with the specific intention for this spell. You might even say a blessing over the water before you start.

When the egg is dry and cool enough, draw a symbol of abundance appropriate to your goal—a flower or other plant, a house, a dollar sign or even the Sun.

Once the symbol is dry, hold the egg in your hands and raise it toward the sky. Say the following (or similar) words:

"As the light and warmth increase,
so does the bounty of my life.
So let it be."

Bury the egg in your garden or somewhere near the front door, visualizing golden light radiating from the egg throughout the soil, nourishing the roots of your growing plants or the foundation of your home.

BELTANE

April 30 or May 1

Oct 31 or Nov 1

Pronounced: bee-YAWL-tinnuh, or BELL-tinnuh

Themes: passion, mischief, sensuality, sexuality, beauty, romance, fertility, vitality, abundance

Also known as: May Day, Walpurgisnacht, Floralia, Calan Mai

By the time May 1st arrives in the Northern Hemisphere, spring is truly in full swing and the balance is tipping toward summer. The heat of the Sun increases with each day, and the Earth turns ever-deepening shades of green as buds and blossoms give way to the emerging new leaves. Flowers seem to explode along the roadsides while birds, bees, and other flying creatures fill the air. And even if a stray chill sneaks back in for a day or two around this time, there's still no going back—winter is decidedly over.

In fact, May 1st marked the official beginning of the light half of the year in pre-modern times, making this day the official beginning of summer for our Celtic ancestors. Indeed, Beltane—or May Day as it is also known—is a time for exuberant celebration, as the long, warm days and the lush abundance of the growing season are ramping up. The hopeful feeling that was kindled at Imbolc and built upon at Ostara now comes into full fruition.

Wiccans recognize Beltane as a time to celebrate the return of passion, vitality, fun and frivolity, and the co-creative energies of Nature that are so evident at this time of year. By this point all living creatures have come out of hibernation and are enjoying the sunshine and the mild days.

"Spring fever" is at its peak, as people find themselves unable to concentrate on their work or studies and long instead to spend all their time outdoors. Primal urges toward lust and wildness become stronger and we see both animals and humans pairing off, sparked by that most basic of instincts: to reproduce.

This life-giving relationship between masculine and feminine energies is honored now, perhaps more directly at this Sabbat than at any other point on the Wheel of the Year. In the cyclical story of the Goddess and the God, this is the shift between their mother-child relationship to that of partners in co-creation.

Over the spring months, the God has matured into his young manhood, and the Goddess is again ready to step from her Maiden aspect into the life-giving Mother. In their prime of life they fall in love and unite, and the Goddess once again becomes pregnant, ensuring the rebirth of the God after the current growing season comes to an end in the autumn.

This is the act that brings about new life in the form of abundant crops, healthy livestock, and forests full of wild game and healing herbs. It is the fundamental building block of the continuation of life, and so is celebrated joyfully at this time by Wiccans and other Pagans alike. In some traditions, the union between the Goddess and God is seen as a divine marriage, and so handfastings—or Wiccan weddings—are customary at this time.

In addition to the Sun God and/or the Horned God, many Wiccans and other Pagans recognize an aspect of the God in the Green Man, an archetypal image of a male face camouflaged by leafy foliage. This mysterious face is found carved into very old buildings throughout Europe, including cathedrals, and is often connected with the Celtic god Cernunnos; however, variations of the image have been discovered all over the world. In early May, as leaves begin to emerge from the trees and shrubs, the return of the Green Man is imminent.

Soon the summer foliage will hide all that was visible during the bare months of winter, and we are reminded of the divinity hidden within plain sight that this greenery so often evokes. Perhaps for this reason, Beltane is also a time of the faeries, who are considered to be more active on this day than any other except for Samhain, which sits directly opposite the Wheel from Beltane.

Faery traditions can be traced back to the Irish *Aos Sí*, a name often translated as "faeries" or "spirits," but are found in various forms throughout ancient pagan cultures. They are said to inhabit various places in Nature, from hills and forests to small plants and flowers. Wiccans who are sensitive to the presence of faeries will leave offerings for them on Beltane Eve.

THE LIGHTING OF THE BALEFIRE

The name "Beltane" has been traced back to an old Celtic word meaning "bright fire," and is thought by some scholars to be related to the ancient Sun god Belenos, whose name has been translated as "bright shining one." Belenos was worshipped throughout Celtic Europe and his feast day was on May 1st, so this connection seems logical, but is not universally accepted by historians.

For one thing, Belenos (also known as Bel or Beil) doesn't make significant appearances in the mythology of the areas where Beltane was historically celebrated: Ireland, Scotland, and the Isle of Mann. In fact, he was much more significant to the Gaulish Celts of the European continent, where the May 1st festivals are known by different names. Nonetheless, the ritual importance of fire was a central focus of Beltane for the ancient Celts of the western-most islands, where the first references to the holiday are found.

The chief event at Beltane in ancient Ireland was the lighting of the balefire on the eve of May 1, the first fire of the light half of the Celtic year. In preparation for this event, every household hearth was extinguished.

Legend has it that tribal representatives from all over Ireland met at the hill of Uisneach, a sacred site where a giant bonfire was lit. Each representative would light a torch from the great fire, and carry it back to their village, where the people waited in the darkness. From the village torch, each household would then relight their home fires, so that all of Ireland was set alight from the same initial flame.

In another version of this story, the fire at Uisneach could be seen from several miles away in every direction, signaling to the surrounding villages to light their own central fires, which was then spread throughout their communities. Either way, this act marked the beginning of summer, with hopes for plentiful sunshine throughout the season.

As a living symbol of the Sun, ritual fire was clearly seen as having magical powers. In many Celtic areas, the Beltane fires were also used for ritual purification of cattle before they were turned out into the summer pastures. The cattle were driven between two large bonfires, which were tended by Druids who used special incantations to imbue the fires with sacred energy.

The fire would clear the animals of any lingering winter disease and protect them from illness and accidents throughout the summer. People would also walk between the fires, or jump over them, for luck and fertility through the coming year. In some areas, the ashes from the smoldering fire would be sprinkled over crops, livestock, and the people themselves.

Over time, the annual Beltane fires grew into larger festivals, where people came to greet each other after the long winter. Dancing, music, games and great feasts became traditions, along with a free license for sexual promiscuity on this special occasion. Other customs observed at this time included eating "Beltane bannock"—a special oatcake that bestowed an abundant growing season and protection of livestock— and making a "May Bush," a branch or bough from a tree decorated with brightly colored ribbons, flowers, and egg shells.

People would dance around the May Bush on Beltane, and then either place it by the front door for luck or burn it in the bonfire. This was believed to be a remnant of Druidic tradition, which held many trees to be sacred and possess magical qualities. A related custom was hanging a rowan branch over the hearth or weaving it into the ceiling to protect the house for the coming year.

Trees, herbs and flowers in general played a part at Beltane and at other May Day celebrations throughout Europe. Primrose flowers and hawthorne and hazel blossoms were gathered and placed at doors and windows, made into garlands, and even used to adorn cattle. Yellow flowers were prized for their association with the Sun.

Herbs gathered on this day were said to be especially potent for magic and healing, especially if gathered at dawn or while the morning dew was still on them. The "May dew" inspired a variety of traditions around beauty. Young women would roll naked in the dew or collect it to wash their faces with, as it was said to purify the skin, maintain youthful looks and help attract a love partner.

CELEBRATING BELTANE

Today's Beltane celebrations draw from various traditions across the pagan landscape of Europe. And while bonfires are definitely a big part of most rituals, Wiccan and other Pagan observances don't necessarily borrow as heavily from Celtic lore at Beltane as they do at Imbolc or Samhain.

More typically, the public celebrations incorporate traditions from Germanic cultures—especially dancing around the Maypole. This is the very tall, circular pole made ideally from wood that features in many May Day festivities, both Pagan and secular alike. At the top of the pole hang ribbons of various colors, and the participants each hold one ribbon as they circle the pole in an interweaving dance, until the length of it is decorated.

This practice is rooted in customs found in England, where the cross-quarter day is known as May Day. The Maypole would be erected in the center of the village, or in a nearby field, and decorated with flowers and branches brought in from the fields, gardens and forests. The villagers would rise at dawn to gather these symbols of summer, and used them to decorate their homes and their bodies as well. Women would braid flowers into their hair, and both men and women—especially those who were young and unmarried—put extra effort into grooming themselves for the big day.

It was traditionally young people who did the dancing around the Maypole, and any woman who wanted to conceive a child was sure to be among them. In the earliest times, the dancing would have been a looser, simpler affair. The more intricately involved dance with the entwining ribbons came about relatively recently, in the 19th century.

Wiccans and other Pagans recognize the pole itself as a supremely phallic symbol, representing the God at the height of his powers. The garlands and greenery symbolize the Goddess and her fertility. As the dancers come together, the ribbons gradually encircle the pole until it is symbolically wrapped in the womb of the Earth. In this way, the union between the divine pair is enacted by the whole community.

This association with phallic symbolism is a somewhat recent development, however. Historians believe that the Maypole originated with fertility rituals of ancient Germanic tribes, who would at one time have been dancing around a young living tree as opposed to a cut pole. The tradition evolved over the centuries after being brought to England, where in the 17th century a mistaken association was made between the Maypole and the bawdier customs of ancient Rome. The phallic symbolism has been part of the lore of May Day ever since, especially among Witches.

Covens have bonfires when possible, often lighting a candle first to represent the 'old fire' of the past seasons. The candle is extinguished, and the bonfire ushers in the 'new fire'—the new energies of the coming year. These energies are typically masculine, but there is also a focus on the cauldron as a symbol of the Goddess.

The gender polarity of Wicca is especially evident at Beltane, and the sexual union of the God and Goddess is symbolically enacted through the joining of the athame with the chalice. Literal coupling—or the Great Rite—is also practiced, though not as commonly. It should be pointed out that as Wicca becomes more expansive, some traditions are less focused on gender polarity in order to accommodate the perspectives of gay and transgender people.

The rich lore surrounding Beltane makes for an abundance of ways to celebrate this Sabbat. A fire is appropriate, whether it's an outdoor bonfire, a small fire in a cauldron or heat resistant bowl, or a host of lit candles. Decorate your altar and your home with green branches and flowers gathered in the early morning, and fill a cauldron or large bowl with water and float fresh blossom petals on top.

It's a good time for beauty rituals, so concoct a facial scrub or mask with dried herbs and fresh water from a stream or spring, or braid your hair to represent the coming together of the Goddess and the God. Make an offering of nuts, berries and fruit for the faeries and leave it under a tree in your yard or in the woods. Tie colored ribbons to young tree branches to make wishes for the coming season. Spend some time with your lover outdoors or work magic to bring a lover into your life. Above all, enjoy the warmth in the air and the accelerating growth of the natural world!

BELTANE CORRESPONDENCES

Colors: light and deep greens, yellow, light blue, red and white for the God and Goddess

Stones: malachite, amber, orange carnelian, sapphire, rose quartz

Herbs: birch trees, hawthorn, honeysuckle, rosemary

Flowers: yellow cowslip, lily of the valley, lilac, hyacinth, daisies, roses

Incense: lilac, frankincense, jasmine, African violet, sage, mugwort

Altar decorations/symbols: Maypole, ribbons, garlands, spring flowers, young plants, Goddess and God statues

Foods: oatmeal cakes, bannock and other bread, dairy foods, strawberries, cherries, spring greens

BELTANE ABUNDANCE DIVINATION

The core theme of Beltane is the fruitful abundance created by the union of the Goddess and the God. You can ask these divine energies for wisdom in helping you manifest your own personal abundance during the coming season.

This is also a great opportunity to deepen your personal relationship with the deities, by simply talking with them in your own words for awhile before pouring the wax. You can use different colors for the deity candles, such as orange and green, if that resonates more with you.

<u>You will need:</u>

- 1 red candle (God)
- 1 white candle (Goddess)
- 1 work candle (optional)
- Small heat-proof plate

<u>Instructions:</u>

Light the work candle, if using.

Place the plate between the two deity candles.

Light the Goddess candle, speaking words of greeting to her as you do so. (You can look up some invocations or simply freestyle it in your own way.)

Light the God candle and greet him in a similar manner.

Spend some time talking to your deities about your hopes for the coming season. Ask any questions you have about any abundance-related issues or developments in your life.

When the candles have accumulated enough melted wax, pick them up together and gently tilt them over the plate, pouring in overlapping circles so that the colors mingle together.

You may want to do this a few times as the candles continue to burn lower. When the wax has dried, look carefully for images and symbols that can point you in the direction of your stated goals.

HERBAL CHARM
FOR FINDING ROMANCE

Beltane is a great time to work magic for new love. This charm is for single people who don't currently have a love prospect in mind. Be careful not to misuse it as a "snare" for someone you have your eye on, or it will backfire!

If you're handy with a needle and thread, you can add power to the charm by sewing your own sachet in the shape of a heart, but the drawstring bag will work just fine.

You will need:

- 1 teaspoon lavender
- 1 teaspoon hibiscus
- 1 teaspoon damiana
- ¼ inch piece cinnamon stick
- Small drawstring bag (ideally red or pink)
- Small piece of rose quartz and/or garnet

Instructions:

Pour the herbs into a small cauldron or bowl.

Mix together with your fingertips to work your personal energy into the herbs.

Stir three times, clockwise, with the cinnamon stick.

Then pour the herb mixture into the bag and add the stones.

As you close up the charm, say the following (or similar) words:

"Herb and stone,
Flesh and bone,
Bring new love
into my home"

Keep the charm in your bedroom, and bring it with you when you go out in public until you meet your next romantic partner.

LITHA (SUMMER SOLSTICE)

Northern Hemisphere: June 20-22

Southern Hemisphere: December 20-23

Pronounced: LEE-tha

Themes: abundance, growth, masculine energy, love, magic

Also known as: Midsummer, Midsummer's Eve, Gathering Day, St. John's Day, St. John's Eve, Summer Solstice, Alban Hefin, Feill-Sheathain

Litha, also known in the wider Pagan world as Midsummer, is celebrated on the day of the Summer Solstice—the longest day and shortest night of the solar year.

This is the height of summer, when the days are warm and plentiful. Abundance can be found everywhere—the crops are in full growth as we get closer to the beginning of the harvest season, and the fields and forests are bursting with animal and plant life.

The Sun reaches its highest point, which means the days will now begin to grow shorter again until we reach the Winter Solstice at Yule. But there's no need to think about winter just now—instead, we celebrate our place on this warm and lively side of the Wheel.

This is the time of the God's greatest power, whether we focus on the light and heat of his Sun God aspect; his role as the Green Man, lush with thick foliage; or the Horned God, strong and agile at the heart of the forest. There is a potent masculine energy to be tapped here, if we wish.

At the same time, the Goddess is in her Mother aspect, as the generous Earth yields abundant blessings of food, flowers, and striking natural beauty. We feel the love of this divine pair easily and often in these easy, breezy days of Midsummer.

Magical and medicinal herbs are said to be at the height of their power, and are traditionally gathered on this day to be dried and stored for use in the winter. Many people also feel the energies of the faeries at this time—a slightly mischievous "something" in the air that Shakespeare once captured in *A Midsummer Night's Dream*.

THE POWER OF THE SUN

Many Pagan sources regarding Litha assert that the Celts celebrated Midsummer in much the same way that they observed their four cross-quarter festivals, but there isn't much evidence to support this idea. Nonetheless, the number of Neolithic stone monuments found throughout Europe that align with the Sun on this day—in both Celtic and non-Celtic lands—indicates that the Summer Solstice was indeed significant to our ancient ancestors.

The most well-known example is Stonehenge in England, where from the center of the circle, the Midsummer Sun can be seen rising over the giant Heel Stone. Today, Pagans of many different traditions gather at Stonehenge on the eve of the Summer Solstice, celebrating throughout the night as they await the sunrise. However, it's unlikely that any of the rituals taking place in modern times are connected to the actual history of Stonehenge.

When it comes to the activities of the ancient Germanic tribes, however, much more is known. Particularly in the northernmost regions of Europe, the solstice would have been great cause for celebration, as the near-endless daylight of the height of summer made for such contrast with the long, dark winters.

In a world without electricity and artificial lighting, the Sun's light would have been unimaginably precious. We can see this in the fire-centered traditions that have come down from Norse, Anglo-Saxon, and other Germanic peoples and are still practiced today. Many of these have inspired the Litha celebrations of Wiccans and other modern Pagans.

Aside from the Sun, and to a lesser extent the Moon, fire was the only source of light available to people until the 19th century. Fire is the symbolic manifestation of the Sun on Earth. It is both tangible and untouchable, miraculous yet dangerous, and it demands respect.

Our pagan ancestors—the Norse in particular—honored the Element of Fire at Midsummer with bonfires and torchlight processions, parading with their families, communities and even animals to their ritual sites for the evening's celebrations. The fires were believed to keep away evil spirits and misfortune. In Anglo-Saxon tradition, boys would roam the fields with their torches to drive away dragons who threatened their springs and wells.

A long-standing tradition in many parts of Europe was the "sunwheel," a giant wagon wheel, tar barrel or ball of straw that was set alight and rolled down a steep hill into a river or other body of water. The significance of this ritual has several possible interpretations. Some suggest it symbolized the annual journey of the Sun—after reaching the zenith of the solstice, it now makes its way back down toward its lowest point at Yule. Others believe it encouraged a natural balance between the Elements of Fire and Water, acknowledging the need for rain to nourish the crops and prevent drought.

The Solstice is still observed today throughout Northern Europe with a variety of rituals dating back to pre-Christian times. Bonfires are held on beaches or near waterways in Denmark and Finland, while in Poland, young girls throw wreaths of flowers into the lakes, rivers, and the Baltic Sea.

In many of these countries, the celebrations begin in the evening and last throughout the night until the Sun rises the following morning. In many places, the day is known as St. John's Day, having been appropriated (like most pagan feasts) by the Christian Church. Nonetheless, the pagan roots of the holiday are still clearly recognizable.

The name "Litha" is a modern innovation, borrowed by Wiccans from an old Saxon word for this time of year. The more traditional

"Midsummer" is also used by many Wiccans and other Pagans, as this date truly falls in the middle of the summer, despite the fact that our modern calendars designate this as the start of the season.

CELEBRATING LITHA

If there's one thing you should definitely put on your Litha "to do" list, it's to get outdoors and enjoy the summer weather! Even if your actual ritual must be held inside, you can prepare yourself energetically by attuning with the Sun's light ahead of time.

It's ideal to spend some time by a river or other body of water, especially if it's a sunny day. Watch the sunrise and the sunset if you can. Many people like to stay up the whole night before in order to see the Sun rise on its most powerful day.

If the weather won't be fair on the solstice day itself, you can commune with Nature the day before or after. But if you're experiencing a string of rainy days, don't fret—the Sun is always there behind the clouds, and you can acknowledge that specifically in your ritual if you wish.

Covens located near a coastline may meet at the shore for their Litha celebrations, in honor of the balance between the Elements of Fire and Water. Rituals are ideally held outdoors, and groups may meet at sunrise on this day, or at "solar noon," the point in the day when the Sun is at its highest in the sky.

One common ritual acts out the story of the battle between the Oak King and the Holly King. In some Wiccan traditions, these twin aspects of the Sun God's annual journey take turns ruling the year. The Oak King, representing the light half of the year, reigns until the Summer Solstice, when he is cut down by the Holly King, who heralds in the beginning of the waning of the light. The ritual enactment serves as a reminder that there can be no light without the dark—it is the contrast between the two that makes each possible.

Magic is, of course, always an appropriate part of Sabbat celebrations, but at Litha the energies available from the abundant natural world are particularly potent. Plug into these currents with spellwork of your choosing. You may want to focus on goals related to love, beauty, friendship, healing, empowerment, or physical and magical energy, but all purposes are suitable at this time.

If you work with the faeries, be sure to acknowledge their presence with offerings of food and/or drink. The height of summer is a great time to watch the subtle movements of the trees in the wind. You just may see a faerie face or two—or even the Green Man himself—among the leaves. If you grow your own herbs, or know how to recognize them in the wild, make a point of gathering a few on this day to use in magical teas, charms, and other workings.

Making protective amulets is a popular magical tradition at this time. Wiccans and other Pagans tie a trio of protective herbs together with cloth to carry or wear around the neck for the coming year. The amulet is charged over the Midsummer bonfire (or a candle if need be). After the year is up, it is buried before a new one is made. Another type of amulet is made with the ashes of the Litha fire, carried in a pouch or kneaded into soft clay that is then baked in a kiln. Litha ashes also make great fertilizer for your garden!

Be sure to incorporate the Element of Fire into your magic, whether with a large ritual bonfire or a few simple candles. If it's a cloudy day, light a candle first thing in the morning and leave it to burn until sunset. This is a good time for clearing and charging crystals and other magical tools by leaving them in sunlight for a few hours. Divination related to love and romance is also traditional at this time, as are rituals of rededication to the God and Goddess.

LITHA CORRESPONDENCES

<u>Colors:</u> gold, green, red, orange, yellow, blue

<u>Stones:</u> emerald, amber, tiger's eye, jade

<u>Herbs:</u> St. John's wort, mugwort, vervain, mint, thyme, chamomile, parsley, oak and holly trees, lavender

<u>Flowers:</u> all flowers, but especially rose, honeysuckle, daisy, lily

<u>Incense:</u> pine, myrrh, rose, cedar, frankincense, lemon, sage, lavender

Altar decorations/symbols: roses, sunflowers, berries, oak and holly leaves, birds, butterflies, sea shells, pinwheels, yellow discs, other solar symbols and imagery

Foods: early summer fruits and vegetables, honey cakes, strawberries, fennel, lemon balm tea, red wine

SUMMER SOLSTICE COURAGE SPELL

With its long days of light and warmth, summer is a time for action and outward-focused energy. This is the perfect time of year to take on a project, enterprise or issue that you've been putting off due to fear of failure or fear of change. Whether you want to ask for a raise, learn to play a new instrument, go back to school, or get to the bottom of a problematic relationship, the energy of the Sun can help you tap into and strengthen your innate courage to dive into the task at hand.

At one point or another, everyone has some fear—whether conscious or unconscious—holding them back from achieving certain goals in life. The fiery essence of the Sun is both purifying and fortifying, allowing you to release your fears and strengthen your sense of well-being regardless of your circumstances.

This is the optimal state of mind from which to approach any kind of challenge, whether your aim is to solve a problem or to enrich your life with a new activity. The Sun card in the Tarot represents power, practicality, freedom and well-being. If you have a Tarot deck, pull out the Sun card and focus on its imagery in preparation for the spellwork.

This spell is suitable any time during the height of summer, but is extra powerful if worked on the day of the Solstice. For spectacular magic, gather your herbs on this day as well, whether you grow them in your garden or purchase them at the market. (You can also see if any of them grow near you in the wild!) Dried herbs will work fine, but in the spirit of lush summer abundance, strive for fresh if possible.

It's ideal to use all four of the herbs included in this spell, which are associated both with courage and with the magical energies of this Sabbat, but if this isn't possible, try to incorporate at least three.

You will need:

- 1 white work candle
- 1 orange spell or votive candle
- 1 teaspoon each of chopped fresh or dried lavender, vervain, St. John's wort and thyme
- Small bowl for mixing herbs
- Small heat-proof plat

- Sun Tarot card (optional)

Instructions:

Light the work candle.

Prop up the Sun card (if using) where you can see it while you work the spell.

Spend a few moments thinking about what it is you want to achieve and how you will feel when you've succeeded.

Hold this feeling in mind as you add the herbs to the bowl, one at a time, mixing them together with your fingertips.

Now hold the orange candle in both hands and charge it with your personal energy.

Visualize yourself outside in full sunlight, basking in the warmth and infused with bright light throughout your entire being. Send this light into the candle.

When you feel ready, place the candle (in a secure holder) on the plate.

Starting at the northernmost point, sprinkle the herbs in a clockwise circle around the base of the candle as you say the following (or similar) words:

> *"As the Sun shines bright at the height of its power,*
> *so my courage comes forth to light the way."*

Now, state your goal out loud as if you've already achieved it. (For example, "*I have enrolled in college classes to advance my career*" or "*I have embarked on a healthier eating plan.*")

Then light the candle and say "*So it is.*"

Leave the candle to burn out on its own.

You can sprinkle the herbs onto the Earth, or burn them in your cauldron.

LITHA ANOINTING OIL

This magical oil can be made at Litha and used year round to harness the powerful energies of the height of summer. Use natural essential oils rather than synthetic fragrance oils if at all possible.

You will need:

- Clean glass jar
- Brown glass bottle
- Small funnel
- 2 tablespoons sunflower oil
- 4 drops lavender oil
- 3 drops lemon oil
- 2 drops cinnamon oil
- 1 drop rose oil

Instructions:

Pour the sunflower oil into a clean glass jar.

Then add one essential oil at a time, taking a moment to inhale the aroma as you swirl the oils together in the jar, building a more and more complex scent as you go.

Funnel your newly-created blend into a brown glass bottle, seal tightly and let it sit outside in the shade for one hour.

If you clear and charge your crystals under the Litha Sun, try anointing them with the oil blend afterward and use them in charms and other spellwork.

LAMMAS

Northern Hemisphere: August 1 or 2

Southern Hemisphere: February 1 or 2

Pronounced: LAH-mahs

Themes: first fruits, harvest, gratitude, benevolent sacrifice, utilizing skills and talents

Also known as: Lughnasa, August Eve, Feast of Bread, Harvest Home, Gŵyl Awst, First Harvest

Situated on the opposite side of the Wheel from Imbolc, which heralds the end of the winter season, Lammas marks the beginning of the end of summer. It is the cross-quarter day between the Summer Solstice and the Autumn Equinox.

Although the days are still hot, sunshine is still abundant and the fields and forests are still teeming with life, we can begin to feel the telltale signs of the approaching autumn. The Sun sets earlier with each passing day, and many plants begin to wither, dropping their seeds to the ground so that new life can return at the start of the next growing season.

Berries, apples, and other fruits begin to ripen on trees and vines, and the grain in the fields has reached its full height, ready to be cut down and stored for the winter. This is a bittersweet time, as we are surrounded by the abundance of the summer's bounty, yet becoming more aware by the day that we are heading back into dark time of year.

Lammas is the time of the "first fruits" and is known in Wiccan and other Pagan traditions as the first of the three harvest festivals. Grain crops are now or soon will be ready for harvesting, along with corn and many other late-summer vegetables and early-autumn fruits. Of course, plenty of produce has already been available for harvesting, and plenty more will be ready later on in the season. But Lammas marks the point in time when harvesting, rather than planting or tending, becomes the main focus.

This is a time to consciously recognize the fruits of our labors—whether literally or metaphorically—and to give thanks for all that has manifested. We recognize the inherent sacrifice of the plants that give their lives so that we may eat, and we are humbled by the greater life-and-death cycles that govern all of creation.

Just six weeks after the Summer Solstice, the God at Lammas is now visibly on the wane. He is approaching his old age, rising later each morning and retiring sooner every night.

The Goddess in her Mother aspect is still waxing, as the Earth continues to bear the fruit of the seeds planted at the start of the growing season. She is still pregnant with the new God, who will be born at Yule, after the old God completes his journey to the Underworld at Samhain. This is one of the most poignant moments on the Wheel of the Year, as the Goddess demonstrates that life goes on even though we all experience loss and the fading of the light.

In ancient agricultural civilizations, grain was often associated with the death and rebirth cycle, and many Wiccan mythological traditions draw on this archetype at Lammas. In one version, the Sun God transfers his power to the living grain in the fields, and so is sacrificed when the grain is cut down. The God willingly sacrifices himself so that his people may live.

And yet the God is later reborn, ensuring that the crops will grow once again to feed the people for another year. The harvest practice of saving seed grain for planting next year's crop is both a practical necessity and a way of participating in the metaphor—saving the seeds is a way of ensuring the God's rebirth.

THE FIRST FRUITS

In the modern world, the first of August is not necessarily an important harvest date, and may seem quite early to some—after all, the summer is still in full swing! In fact, due to our advanced agricultural technology, there are now actually multiple growing cycles for various types of grain and other crops.

But back when harvesting, threshing, winnowing and sieving of the grain was all done by hand, farmers needed to start as early as they could. After all, once this hard work was done, it would be time to bring in the later-season crops ahead of the first killing frosts.

Of course, August 1st wasn't necessarily a hard and fast date for our ancestors, though it was considered the earliest acceptable time to begin bringing in the wheat. But if the crop wasn't quite ready, due to insufficient rain or sunshine, then the harvest—and the accompanying festivities—would wait. Nature's schedule was far more powerful than any calendar humans could devise.

Although the harvesting process meant long hours of hard work for the farmers, it was still cause for celebration and merriment. Many families' stores of wheat would have run very low or even empty by this time, and the onset of the harvest season meant that plenty of new abundance was on its way.

It was also a very social time, as neighbors worked together in order to bring the harvest in successfully for everyone in the community. Feasting was a must, and a special emphasis was placed on bread, as a staple of nourishment that would provide for the family throughout the long winter months and beyond.

The first loaves made from the first wheat of the new season were particularly significant, and in Anglo-Saxon England, these loaves were brought into the churches and laid on the altar to be blessed. This is where the holiday gets its name—the old Saxon phrase "hlaf-maesse," which translates literally to "loaf mass," and eventually became "Lammas."

The custom of blessing the bread makes Lammas an interesting example of how Christianity and pagan religions coexisted for a time.

Bread is actually an important symbol in many spiritual traditions, going back to the ancient world.

For Wiccans and other modern Pagans, bread is representative of all the Elements: the seeds growing in the Earth, the yeast utilizing Water and Air to make the dough rise, and the Fire of the hearth making the finished product. Add to this the concept of Akasha—or Spirit—being present in the grain thanks to the power of the Sun, and you have a very sacred food indeed.

Given the significance of bread to the communion rituals of the Christian Church, it's easy to see how these traditions overlapped. But if the Church officials had hoped to stomp out pagan practices with the "loaf mass," they didn't succeed, at least not immediately—the Anglo-Saxon peasants were known to use their church-blessed bread in protection rituals and other magic.

As an agricultural festival, the First Harvest would certainly have preceded the arrival of Christianity to Europe. And yet it's unknown what this holiday was called in England prior to the custom that brought about the name of "Lammas." However, in Ireland the day was, and still is, known as Lughnasa (pronounced "LOO-na-sa" or "Loo-NOSS-ah," also spelled "Lughnasadh").

This cross-quarter festival was held as a tribute to the Celtic God Lugh, a warrior deity who was associated with the Sun, fire, grain, and many skills and talents such as smithcraft, building, music and magic. The association with grain comes from Lugh's foster mother, Tailtiu, who was said to have cleared the plains of Ireland for use in agriculture and died of exhaustion from doing so.

Lugh held an annual harvest festival in her honor, which included athletic games and contests that resembled the original Olympics, along with music and storytelling. This mythical festival was made real by the ancient Celts and was celebrated in one form or another well into the 20th century.

As with other ancient harvest festivals, Lughnasa was a time to offer the "first fruits" to the gods. The first of the crops were carried to the top of a high hill and buried there. Bilberries were gathered and a sacred bull was sacrificed for the great feast.

Ritual plays were performed in which Lugh defeated blight or famine and seized the harvest for the people. Dancing, drinking, trading and matchmaking were popular activities at the gatherings, which might last for three days before coming to a close. Handfastings and trial marriages (which lasted a year and a day and could then be broken or made permanent) were also common, as were visits to holy wells, where people would pray for good health and leave offerings of coins or strips of cloth.

CELEBRATING LAMMAS

Across the spectrum of Wiccan and other modern Pagan traditions, celebrations at Lammas can vary widely. Those inspired by the ancient Celts may choose to focus on honoring Lugh, and many call this holiday Lughnasa rather than Lammas. Others might be more rooted in Anglo-Saxon traditions, while still others incorporate a blend of ancient sources into their practice. Among all this diversity, however, the central theme is almost always the first harvest and the beginning of the transition into the darker, colder months.

Feasts are part of every Sabbat, but the significance of the feast is a particular focus during the harvest holidays, as we give thanks to the God and Goddess for the bounty of the Earth. Wiccans deliberately choose to prepare and savor the first "fruits" of the harvest season, whether it be apples and grapes, wheat and corn, or anything else that has come into season where they live. This feast is a physical participation in the turning of the Wheel of the Year, as we recognize that this time of newly-reaped abundance, like all other moments in time, will soon pass.

Coven rituals at Lammas often honor the waxing energy of the pregnant Goddess and the waning energy of the fading God. They give thanks for the manifestations of the year thus far, whether material, spiritual, or both. In some traditions, goals for the next two harvest Sabbats are stated, as well as intentions for the bounty of the Earth to be shared by all beings.

For solitary practitioners, a full-scale feast may be somewhat impractical, especially for those who live alone. If this is the case, you can still make a point of enjoying some fresh baked bread and late-summer fruits and vegetables as part of your Lammas celebration. Save any seeds from the fruits for planting, or use them in your spellwork.

Another way to mark this Sabbat is to make a corn dolly from corn stalks or straw. This is a manifestation of the ancient "Corn Mother" archetype found around the world. She can be placed on your altar and even used in magic. Since crafting is a way of honoring the Celtic god Lugh at this time, consider making and/or decorating other ritual items, such as a wand or pentacle.

You could also choose to practice any of your skills and talents, whether that means writing, playing an instrument, playing in a soccer or basketball game, or simply going for a nice long run. If there's a new skill you'd like to learn, now is a great time to get started.

Whatever you do, be sure to spend some time outdoors drinking in the sights, sounds, and smells of summer because they will be fading away before you know it!

LAMMAS CORRESPONDENCES

<u>Colors:</u> gold, yellow, orange, red, green, light brown
Stones: carnelian, citrine, peridot, aventurine, sardonyx

<u>Herbs:</u> sage, meadowsweet, ginseng, vervain, calendula, fenugreek, heather, dill, yarrow

<u>Flowers:</u> sunflower, passionflower, acacia flowers, cyclamen

<u>Incense:</u> sandalwood, frankincense, copal, rose, rose hips, rosemary, chamomile, passionflower

<u>Altar decorations/symbols:</u> first harvest fruits and vegetables, fresh baked bread, grapes and vines, corn dollies, sickles and scythes, Lugh's spear, symbols representing your own skills

<u>Foods:</u> apples, breads, all grains, berries, hazelnuts, summer squash, corn, elderberry wine, ale

LAMMAS GRATITUDE
AND BREAD BLESSING RITUAL

As anyone who practices gratitude on a regular basis will tell you, it really pays to express appreciation for the blessings in your life. This is because of the Law of Attraction—the more you appreciate, the more you attract new things and circumstances to appreciate!

But it's also good to express gratitude simply for its own sake. Any Sabbat is an excellent occasion to do so, but it's especially appropriate at Lammas, the season of the first fruits.

This ritual provides a simple, elegant structure for thanking the God and Goddess, Nature, or whatever your term may be for the powers that govern the Universe. If seven candles are too much to manage for whatever reason, you can certainly use fewer, but it's nice to get a little decadent with this if you can.

You will need:

- 7 gold, yellow and orange candles (any size and in any combination)
- Handful of fresh sunflower and/or calendula petals
- Loaf of fresh-baked bread
- Pen (or pencil) and writing paper

Instructions:

Arrange the candles and sprinkle the petals among them in a manner that pleases you.

Place the bread in front of the candles and light one of them.

Now, make a list of at least 10 blessings you've experienced over the past few months. These can be hugely significant or "little things." Usually, it will be a combination of both. You will likely find that more and more things occur to you as you write (again, the Law of Attraction at work).

When you've got a good list together, light the rest of the candles and then read the list aloud, starting with "*Thank you for...*" before each item.

Now, hold the bread up toward the sky and say the following (or similar) words:

"God and Goddess, I thank you for this bread, which represents all the blessings I have listed here and more. May all on Earth be nourished by the bounty of Nature. So let it be."

Eat some of the bread, and be sure to use the rest of it over the coming days.

SKILL-BUILDING CRYSTAL CHARM

In the spirit of Lugh, the god of many skills, this simple charm can support you in developing or strengthening any skill, whether it's related to work or leisure. You can use any crystal or mineral stone you feel an affinity with, but choosing one with Lammas/Lughnasa associations makes for a nice extra boost at this time of year.

Corresponding crystals include:

Aventurine: confidence, creativity, luck
Citrine: joy, success
Sardonyx: strength, willpower

You will need:

- 1 small-to-medium-sized crystal
- 1 red or yellow candle
- Rosemary, cinnamon, or other "activating" essential oil

Instructions:

Anoint the candle and the crystal with the oil.

Hold the crystal in your dominant hand and feel its energies moving through you.

Visualize yourself being highly proficient in your chosen skill.

Hold this feeling in your heart as you light the candle.

Place the crystal in front of the candle and allow the candle to burn out on its own.

Keep your crystal with you whenever you're practicing your skill, and rub it with your thumb whenever you need a little boost of confidence.

MABON
(AUTUMN EQUINOX)

Northern Hemisphere: September 21-24

Southern Hemisphere: March 20-22

Pronounced: MAY-bun, MAH-bun, MAY-vhon, or MAH-bawn

Themes: harvest, gratitude, abundance, balance, preparation, welcoming the dark

Also known as: Autumnal Equinox, Fall Equinox, September Equinox, Harvest Tide, Harvest Home, Harvest Festival, Wine Harvest, Feast of Avalon, Alben Elfed, Meán Fómhair, Gwyl canol Hydref

Mabon is the name used by Wiccans and many other modern Pagans for the Sabbat falling at the Autumn Equinox. Compared to the solstices, which actually occur during the middle of their respective seasons, the equinoxes mark more significant shifts from one season to the next.

By this point on the Wheel, the end of summer has become undeniable—a crisp chill in the air descends each evening at sunset, and the leaves on deciduous trees have begun to turn deep, bright shades of red, yellow and orange. The blue of the afternoon sky deepens as the summer's white-hot sunlight turns golden. Plant life dies back in gardens, fields and forests, and squirrels get busy gathering acorns and walnuts to stash away for the coming cold months.

For many people, this is a bittersweet moment, as the beauty of the transforming Earth reminds us that we're heading into bleak and barren times. But this is the true essence of the seasons and the Wheel—all of creation is always in motion, and the only constant in life is change.

The cyclical nature of time is especially apparent at Mabon as we work with themes that echo both Lammas and Ostara. Mabon is the second of the three harvest festivals, representing the pinnacle of abundance when it comes to the crops of the fields and the bounty of our gardens. Once again, we take time to appreciate all we have manifested—material and otherwise—through our efforts over the past several months.

There is more to do between now and Samhain to prepare for the winter, and this is a good time to take stock and evaluate what plans and projects need to be brought to completion before we enter the dark half of the year. But it's also a moment to pause and celebrate what has taken place thus far.

In doing so, we give thanks to those who have assisted us, whether they be friends, family, or spirit guides and ancestors on the other side. And we recognize the importance of sharing our good fortune with others, by hosting feasts as well as giving to those in need.

The other central focus at this time is balance. Like Ostara, which falls on the Spring Equinox, Mabon marks the point at which day and night are of equal length. This time, the Sun crosses the "celestial equator" and appears to head south. From now until Yule, the light will wane significantly, with the nights becoming noticeably longer than the days. However, at this moment, the light and the dark are balanced.

Interestingly, the Autumn Equinox coincides with the Sun's entrance into the Zodiac sign of Libra. Libra's symbol is the scales, and it is the sign known for seeking balance, harmony and equality. However much some of us may prefer warmth to cold or light to dark (or vice versa), we also know that without their opposites, we couldn't truly appreciate our favorite times of year. Participating in the turning of the Wheel through ritual and celebration helps us live in harmony with these shifting tides.

This recognition of the necessity of change—more specifically, the necessity of death in the life/death/rebirth cycle—is seen in the shifting relationship between the Goddess and the God. At Mabon, neither is young anymore.

The aging God is even further weakened than at Lammas, and will soon give way completely to the dominance of the dark at Samhain. The Goddess is still in her Mother aspect as the Earth continues to bear fruit, and she still holds the new God in her womb. Yet she is moving toward her Crone aspect as well, where she will reign alone over the dark, mysterious nights until the God is reborn at Yule.

The bittersweet quality of this time of year is embodied by the Goddess herself, who mourns the passing of the God yet knows he will return anew. In some traditions, the Goddess actually follows the God to the Underworld, which is why the Earth becomes cold and barren. In others, it is her sadness at his absence that causes the leaves to fall, the plants to die, and the animals to slumber away in hidden shelters. Still others view the coming weeks simply as a time of needed rest for all of the Earth, the equal and balanced opposite of the active energy of spring.

THE HORN OF PLENTY

While the Autumn Equinox was celebrated in several places throughout Asia, there's little evidence to suggest that the ancient pagans of Europe marked this specific day with any major fanfare. However, harvest festivals were widely observed at some point during the fall season in many cultures.

In the areas comprising what is now the United Kingdom, the traditional harvest festival was tied to both the solar and lunar calendars, being held around the Full Moon closest to the Autumn Equinox. And the remains of ancient neolithic sites throughout Britain and Ireland which were designed to align with the Sun on this day show that it was considered an important moment to observe and honor.

This lack of historical information made the Autumn Equinox somewhat difficult to give a unique name to, at least compared to the other solar Sabbats. In the early 1970s, the name "Mabon" was suggested by Aidan Kelly, a prominent member of the growing Pagan community in the U.S.

Mabon is the name of a Welsh mythological figure who is mentioned in Arthurian legends. He is considered a deity by some, but not enough is known about him to confirm this status, as many figures in ancient pagan myths are the children of unions between deities and humans. Nonetheless, Mabon is the son of the goddess Modron, who is often described as the primordial triple goddess of the ancient Celts. The story we have of Mabon is that he was abducted from his mother when he was three days old, and held imprisoned in a secret location into adulthood, until he is rescued by King Arthur's men.

In actuality, "Mabon" means "son," and "Modron" means "mother," so we don't really know whether these two mythical figures had specific names. Yet these archetypes are somewhat fitting for a Wiccan Sabbat in that they echo the mother-child relationship of the God and Goddess.

As the mythology and symbolism of the Wheel of the Year has evolved, the tale of Mabon has grown into something new, with various writers borrowing elements of ancient myths from other cultures, especially the Greeks and the Norse. In one version, Modron's grief over her missing son is given as the reason for the turning of the season—her sadness causes darkness and cold to envelop the Earth. In another, it is Mabon's imprisonment deep within the ground that leads to the turning inward of animals and plant life.

As with Ostara, we can see that the lore around Mabon is rather more modern than that of most other Sabbats. Nonetheless, the sorrow inherent to the original tale can be seen as appropriate for this time of year, as the absence of light looms closer and closer.

If Ostara's symbols are the hare and the egg, then the chief symbol of Mabon is the cornucopia, also known as "the horn of plenty." This image—a large, hollowed-out horn filled to overflowing with fruits and vegetables—is widely recognized in North America as part of the modern "harvest festival" of Thanksgiving. However, it was part of the harvest festivals of Europe for many centuries before making its way to the new world.

The word "cornucopia" comes from the Latin words for "horn" and "plenty," but the symbol itself goes back even further to the ancient

Greeks. It features prominently in Greek mythology, particularly in a story about Zeus as an infant. His supernatural strength caused him to accidentally break off one of the horns of Amalthea, the goat who watched over him and fed him with her milk. The severed horn then gained the power to provide infinite nourishment.

Other deities associated with the cornucopia include the Greek goddesses Gaia (the Earth) and Demeter (a grain goddess) and the Roman goddess Abundantia (the personification of abundance). As we can see, the cornucopia is a very fitting symbol for this Wiccan Sabbat—not just because of its pagan origins, but also because of its association with the Horned God.

CELEBRATING MABON

The cornucopia is an excellent place to start when it comes to your own Mabon celebration. You can make your own completely from scratch or buy a horn-shaped basket and fill it with fresh autumn produce, nuts, herbs, flowers and even crystals to place on your altar.

Use it in ritual to express gratitude for the abundance in your life, and/or in spellwork for abundance and prosperity. You can also leave it outdoors at night as an offering to the animals and faeries, and bury whatever isn't eaten by the end of the following day. The cornucopia also makes an excellent gift and a way for you to share the bounty in your life with others.

Coven rituals at Mabon often focus on balance and on giving thanks for life's blessings, particularly those that have come to pass over the past several months. New or continuing goals may be identified for the next and final harvest at Samhain. The Mabon feast is particularly lavish as we are at the height of the harvest season. Food is often shared with shelters and other organizations on behalf of the less fortunate.

There is also an acknowledgment of the coming dark, with thanks given to the retreating Sun. In some traditions, it is time to actively welcome the dark, and to honor spirits and aging deities—especially Crone goddesses—in preparation for Samhain.

For Witches who tend gardens, now is the time to harvest what is ready, tend what is still growing, and collect and save seeds for next year's crops. You might make an offering to nature spirits with some of your bounty, or offer seeds, grains and acorns or cider.

Be sure to spend quality time outdoors, drinking in the last of the sunshine. Gather brightly colored leaves to place on your altar, and give thanks to the Goddess and God for the graceful beauty with which they bring the light half of the year to a close. For spellwork, consider goals related to harmony and balance, as well as protection, prosperity, and self-confidence.

MABON CORRESPONDENCES

<u>Colors:</u> deep reds, maroon, orange, yellow, gold, bronze, brown

<u>Stones:</u> amber, topaz, citrine, tiger's eye, lapis lazuli, sapphire, yellow agate

<u>Herbs:</u> chamomile, milkweed, thistle, yarrow, saffron, hops, Solomon's seal, sage, rue, hazel, ivy, oakmoss, mace

<u>Flowers:</u> marigold, sunflower, rose, aster, chrysanthemum

<u>Incense:</u> benzoin, cedar, pine, myrrh, frankincense, sandalwood, cinnamon, clove, sage

<u>Altar decorations/symbols:</u> cornucopia, gourds, acorns, pine cones, pinwheels, yellow discs, other solar symbols and imagery

<u>Foods:</u> nuts, wheat and other grains, bread, grapes, apples, pumpkin, pomegranate, all autumn fruits and vegetables, wine

MABON FLOATING CANDLE SPELL

Mabon, like its "twin" Ostara, is a time to reflect on harmony and balance. But whereas the Spring Equinox is focused on balance in your relationship with the outer world, the Autumn Equinox asks you to turn your focus inward.

What aspects of your relationship with yourself could use some balancing? Are you open and listening to your own inner guidance, or are you letting the opinions of others get in the way? Are you speaking kindly to and about yourself or are you always being your own harshest critic? What nagging thoughts or emotions might you be in the habit of ignoring or stuffing down?

Traditionally, Autumn is associated with the Element of Water, which rules the psychic and emotional tides that ebb and flow between our conscious and unconscious selves. This spell makes use of the theme of balance with a candle floating in a cauldron. Use it as a portal to strengthen your inner balance for the coming season, and as a way of preparing for any shadow work you'd like to take on at Samhain.

You will need:

- 1 work candle
- 1 white floating candle
- Small cauldron or bowl
- Marigold or sunflower petals

Instructions:

Light the work candle.

Fill the cauldron with water up to about 1/2 inch from the top.

Sprinkle the flower petals on the water's surface, and gently float the candle among the petals.

Spend some time journaling about any inner conflicts or questions you'd like to harmonize within yourself. Try to write for at least 20 minutes.

When you feel you've hit on a particular aspect of yourself that could use some balancing at this time, write a short phrase or draw a symbol that represents it.

Light the floating candle as you keep this phrase or symbol in your third eye.

Sit quietly for a few moments and take in the sight of the flame, the water, and the petals.

You may wish to resume writing and/or stay open for any insights that come to you regarding your issue.

Leave the candle to burn out on its own.

AUTUMN PROTECTION CHARM

This charm can be used at any time of year, but it's especially appropriate for the autumn season when the impending darkness can start to get slightly under your skin.

Keep negativity at bay with a combination of herbs and minerals from the Earth. Each of the stones and herbs below are used in protection magic. Select those that resonate with you most for a personalized charm. For optimal protective powers, use at least two of the three herbs listed below.

<u>You will need:</u>
- Small drawstring bag
- 1-2 pieces of tiger's eye, amber, and/or carnelian
- 1 tablespoon each of sage, chamomile, and/or yarrow

<u>Instructions:</u>

Charge your ingredients in direct sunlight for one hour.

As you place them in the drawstring bag, visualize yourself surrounded by golden light.

Carry the charm with you whenever you feel highly energetically sensitive.

SAMHAIN

Northern Hemisphere: October 31 or November 1

Southern Hemisphere: April 30 or May 1

Pronounced: SOW-in, SAH-vin, or SOW-een

Themes: death, rebirth, divination, honoring ancestors, introspection, benign mischief, revelry

Also known as: Samhuin, Oidhche Shamhna, Halloween, Third Harvest, Day of the Dead, Feast of the Dead (Félie Na Marbh), Shadowfest, Ancestor Night, Feile Moingfinne (Snow Goddess), Winter Nights, Old Hallowmas, Calan Gaeaf

Of all the Sabbats, Samhain is considered to be the most powerful and important to Wiccans and other Witches, with many intense energies at play. This is when we honor the Death element of the life/death/rebirth cycle that forms the basis of the Wheel of the Year and all of Nature as we know it.

Wiccans understand that the death stage of the cycle is actually the most potent, as it is here that all potential for new life resides, waiting to be manifested into specific form.

Therefore, Samhain is the most fitting time for reflecting on our lives, looking back over the past year and identifying any circumstances or patterns of behavior we would like to allow to die, in order to make room for the new when the growing season begins again. By letting go of our old selves, we can move into the winter months ahead with clarity and acceptance of the ever-turning wheel of life and death.

The name "Samhain" has been translated from the Old Irish as "summer's end," and this date marked the beginning of the dark half of the year in the ancient Celtic world. This is the third and final harvest festival, the time to stock the root cellars with the last of the winter squashes, turnips, beets and other root vegetables, and to dry the last of the magical and medicinal herbs for winter storage.

The fields are now empty of their crops, the once-green meadow grasses are dying back to gold and brown, and the leaves have peaked and fallen, leaving the trees bare and stark against the greying skies. The chill in the air that began with Mabon is now here to stay, and the weakened Sun gives barely a passing glance for a few short hours before descending again below the horizon.

Indeed, it can seem as if the world is dying at this time. But this feeling is alleviated by the gratitude we express for all the abundance of the past year, and the knowledge that the light will return again, as is promised by the Wheel.

The perpetual life/death/rebirth cycle is characterized by both the God and the Goddess at Samhain.

In his Sun aspect, the God has aged considerably since Mabon. His power is nearly gone, and he descends into the Underworld, leaving the Earth to the darkness of winter. As the Horned God, or the God of the Hunt, he is a fully matured stag who gives his life so his people can survive the coming barren season. Wiccans say farewell to the God at this Sabbat, thanking him for fulfilling his life-sustaining roles over the past year and expressing faith that he will return, reborn, at Yule.

In many traditions, the Goddess is said to be mourning the God at this time, yet she too knows that he will return, as she is now in her wise Crone aspect. From the aged Crone we learn that death is part of life, that the old must be released in order for us to learn, grow, and birth new manifestations.

It is interesting that the Goddess herself never dies, since the Earth remains steadily present throughout the year, no matter where the Sun may be. Yet she represents death and life simultaneously—she is both Crone and mother-to-be of the new God.

SPIRITS AND SYMBOLS

For the Celts, from whom the name and many customs of this Sabbat are borrowed, Samhain was something of a dark mirror to Beltane—a counterpart of sorts which sits directly opposite the Wheel.

Once again, it was time to move the cattle, only now they were brought back to their winter pastures. The ritual bonfires and great gatherings that celebrated fertility in May were now a recognition of the abundance manifested throughout the light half of the year.

This was the time to gather the last harvest of the apples and nuts, and to select the animals that would be slaughtered to feed the people for the coming months. The meat would be salted and stored for the winter, and the bones from the Samhain feast were thrown upon the fires as offerings to secure good fortune for the next season's cattle. (This tradition gives us the word "bonfire"—"bone + fire.")

The gatherings at Samhain were festive affairs, as people danced, drank, feasted, and traded goods for the last time before winter kept everyone close to home. It was clearly an important time, as many key tales in early Irish mythology occur at Samhain.

As the first day of winter and the beginning of the dark half of the year, Samhain was, like its Beltane counterpart, a time of open passageways between the world of the living and the Otherworld, or world of the spirit. However, whereas Beltane focused on summer and the bursting forth of life that warmth and sunshine bring, Samhain was an acknowledgment of the cold, the dying back of the Earth, and the dead themselves who have gone before us.

Samhain Eve was, like Beltane Eve, a time of heightened activity on the part of the Aos Sí, or faeries, who were said to be extra mischievous now. These supernatural beings were to be steered clear of, to the extent that people avoided being out of doors on this night. If they had to leave home, they would carry iron or salt to discourage the Aos Sí from coming near. It was also believed that the Aos Sí needed to be appeased in order to ensure that the family and its livestock survived the coming winter, so offerings of food and drink were left for the faeries outside the door of the house.

With the Otherworld so easily accessible, Samhain was also a time for honoring the dead, who were thought to wander about and visit their family homes, seeking a warm welcome and a meal. The Samhain feast always included a place at the table reserved for the ancestors, and room was also left for them by the hearth. To make sure their loved ones could find their way, a single candle was lit in each window of the house. People also left apples along the roadsides for spirits who had no living relatives to welcome them.

In general, it was believed that the dead, like the Aos Sí, had to be appeased at this time or misfortune might fall upon the family. However, blessings could be bestowed by appreciative departed souls as well. This belief in the need to placate the dead is found in ancient cultures around the world, and is seen most explicitly today in the Mexican Day of the Dead, which begins on October 31 and has roots in both European and Aztec cultures.

Since the spirit world was so readily accessible at Samhain, divination was a popular activity during the festival. Many different forms were practiced, often to discover information about future marriages or deaths. People's names were marked on stones which were then thrown into the bonfire. These would be plucked from the ashes the next day and "read" according to the condition they were in.

Crows and other birds were counted as they passed in the sky, with their number or direction being assigned specific meanings. Apples and nuts were often used in divination games. One popular activity was peeling an apple in one unbroken strip, casting the peel onto the floor, and reading the shape to find the first letter of the name of one's future spouse.

Another tradition evolved into what we now know as "bobbing for apples." In Celtic mythology, the apple was associated with immortality and the Otherworld. Hazelnuts were associated with divine wisdom, and were chewed by Druids in Scottish myths in order to gain prophecies.

There are many aspects of our modern Halloween celebrations that have their roots in Samhain customs. The fear of faeries and spirits roaming the night led our Celtic ancestors to disguise themselves in white, as if to blend in with the ghosts, or wear costumes made of straw to confuse them. This evolved into the tradition of "guising," in which people dressed in disguise to represent the spirits of the night and travelled from house to house collecting gifts of apples, nuts and other food for the Samhain feast.

In Scotland in particular, it was common for those imitating the mischievous faeries to play pranks on their neighbors, especially if they did not receive an offering from the household. These original "trick-or-treaters" carried lanterns made from hollowed-out turnips, which were often carved with frightening faces to either represent or ward off evil spirits. The lanterns were also left on windowsills or doorsteps to protect the home on Samhain Eve, a custom which later evolved into our modern "jack-o-lanterns."

Other symbols of Halloween which may have originated with the Celts include the skull and the skeleton. The skull was revered by Celtic warriors as the house of the soul and the seat of one's power, and it is thought that skulls were used as oracles. Skeleton imagery, seen particularly in Day of the Dead celebrations, is traced by some back to ancient Europe.

A classic symbol of Halloween is, of course, the Witch and all of her associated imagery—the broom, the cauldron and the black cat. Of course, this link stems from the misguided fear of "evil witches" promoted by the Christian Church in later centuries, but nonetheless it can be attributed to the connection that these shamanic practitioners had to the world of spirit.

There's a nice bit of irony here, in that Samhain—the "Witch's holiday"— seems to be the one that the Church just couldn't stamp out. For although November 1 was converted to "All Saints' Day," the old pagan trappings of the original festival remain alive and well, even in mainstream culture.

CELEBRATING SAMHAIN

For Wiccans and other Pagans, Samhain is very much rooted in the ancient Celtic traditions. It is often described as the night when "the veil between the worlds is at its thinnest," and many choose to honor their ancestors and other departed loved ones at this time. Food and drink are left out for any wandering spirits, and many Witches seek communication with the Other Side.

We do not fear mischief or retribution from the dead, as we know our ancestors don't mean us harm, but we do honor and respect their presence. The Wiccan belief in reincarnation is also meditated upon at Samhain, as we recognize that the life/death/rebirth cycle applies to all living beings. We know that we do not return to the Other Side permanently, but rest and enjoy ourselves there until we're ready to be reborn into the physical world.

Samhain is a key occasion for divination of all kinds, including scrying, Tarot, runes and I-Ching, as well as various uses of apples. For those who work with the faeries, this is definitely an important night to leave offerings for them!

In many traditions, Samhain is also considered the start of the new year, as it is believed that the Celtic year began on the evening of October 31st. Scholars disagree about whether there is sufficient evidence for this, but Samhain is listed in Irish medieval literature as the first of the four cross-quarter day festivals, so the association has stuck.

Whether your tradition considers the year to begin now or at Yule, however, Samhain is an excellent time to reflect on your life and any changes you wish to make during the year ahead. This is the time in between death and new life, as the Crone/Mother Goddess waits for the God to be reborn.

What in your personal world do you wish to allow to die, and what new developments would you like to give birth to? What has ended that you need to fully let go of in order to make room for the new?

Coven rituals at Samhain are often held outdoors, at night, around a sacred bonfire. The coven members may focus on letting go of bad habits and other unwanted energies, symbolically releasing them into the fire to be transformed. Other ritual themes may include bidding farewell to the Old God, tapping into the wisdom of the Crone, and formally honoring the dead.

And of course, any Wiccans who practice spellwork are certain to do so on this night, the most potent time of the entire year for magic! Any type of work is bound to be effective, but in keeping with the themes of this Sabbat, goals related to banishing, releasing, and strengthening your psychic abilities are especially appropriate.

On your Samhain altar, include photographs or mementos from deceased loved ones and light a votive candle specifically for them. Since this is the Sabbat most associated with Witchcraft, include symbols like cauldrons, besoms (ritual brooms), and pentacles, even if you don't necessarily work with these tools regularly. As always, seasonal decorations of all kinds are key, but try to include a pumpkin if you can—carved and illuminated if possible!

Finally, be sure to give your sacred space a very thorough sweeping before beginning any ritual or spellwork. As you clean, visualize all unwanted energies and influences from the past year being swept away and out of your life.

SAMHAIN CORRESPONDENCES

<u>Colors:</u> black, orange, rust, bronze, brown, grey, silver, gold

<u>Stones:</u> jet, obsidian, onyx, smoky quartz, all other black stones, bloodstone, carnelian

<u>Herbs:</u> mugwort, wormwood, valerian, rosemary, sage, catnip, broom, oak leaves, witch hazel, angelica, deadly nightshade*, mandrake*,

<u>Flowers:</u> marigold, chrysanthemums, sunflower, goldenrod, Russian sage, pansies

<u>Incense:</u> nutmeg, mint, sage, copal, myrrh, clove, heather, heliotrope, benzoin, sweetgrass, sandalwood

<u>Altar decorations/symbols:</u> oak leaves and other fallen leaves, pomegranates, pumpkins, squashes, gourds, photos or other tokens of deceased loved ones, acorns, Indian corn, besom, cauldron

<u>Foods:</u> pumpkins, pomegranates, apples, all root vegetables and autumn/winter squashes, all nuts, breads, beans, apple cider, mulled cider, ale, herbal teas

*These herbs are highly toxic and should be used with care in spellwork only. Do not ingest!

SPELL TO END A BAD HABIT

With its emphasis on banishing and the death of the old, Samhain is a perfect opportunity to get some magical assistance with releasing any habit you want to be free of. The only caveat is that you have to *want* to end the habit. Without that motivation, this spell is unlikely to succeed.

You will need:

- 1 work candle (optional)
- 1 black candle
- 5 pieces of jet, obsidian, onyx, smokey quartz, and/or black tourmaline
- Small square of paper
- Pen or pencil (or ink and quill)
- Cauldron or other heat-proof dish

Instructions:

Light the work candle, if using.

Arrange the stones around the cauldron in a pentagram shape.

Light the black candle and sit quietly, imagining the freedom and vitality you will experience with this habit gone from your life.

When you're ready, write the habit on the square of paper.

Holding it in your dominant hand, raise it over the candle flame and say the following (or similar) words:

> *"As the fire burns among these stones*
> *I ask the blessings of the Crone:*
> *Release this habit written here*
> *without judgement, without fear."*

Now ignite the paper with the flame. (Be careful not to burn your fingers!)

When it's burning enough to incinerate completely, drop it into the cauldron.

Take the ashes outside and sprinkle them onto the Earth.

Allow the candle to burn out on its own.

Bury the stones or throw them in a creek or river to cast away all remaining traces of the habit.

SPIRIT-GUIDED WRITING

Automatic writing is a very effective way to channel insights and advice from the spirit realm. Each of us has guides on the Other Side with wisdom to share if we only tap into their energies.

If you write in a journal regularly, you have most likely already received information from the spirit world, in the form of inspired thoughts that seem to flow out of the pen without effort. Automatic writing is similar, only you're deliberately asking for the words to come through you, without your conscious mind making any decisions about the content or otherwise interfering in the process.

If writing at your altar isn't practical, transform a desk or table into your sacred space for this work. Be sure to ground and center yourself by meditating, taking a ritual bath, or any other activity that helps you connect with your own highest energy.

Opening yourself up to spirit energy can be disorienting and even unpleasant if you're not properly grounded, so it's especially important to prepare yourself energetically before you begin.

You will need:

- 1 white candle
- Mugwort
- Sage bundle
- Quartz crystal
- Amethyst
- Journal or sheets of paper
- Pen or pencil

Instructions:

Light the candle, and place the quartz and amethyst on either side of it.

Use the flame to ignite the sage, and smudge yourself and your surroundings to clear away any unwanted energy.

Take a few deep breaths and say the following (or similar) words:

*"I surround myself in love and light
and seek my spirits' guidance tonight.
Guardians wise and helpers sage,
Speak truth to me through pen and page."*

To prime the psychic connection between you and your guides, gently rub mugwort over the front and back of your journal (or on the first and last sheets of paper).

Then take up your pen (or pencil) and begin writing whatever comes to mind.

It may take a little while before your conscious mind lets go and the words begin to feel that they're coming from outside of you. If you like, you can write down a question to get started, but don't be surprised if what comes through is on a different topic altogether—you're asking for what the Universe most wants you to know at this time.

Write for at least 10 to 15 minutes. Remember, don't pay conscious attention to what you're writing—instead, let your eyes focus softly on your hand, your pen, or the candle as you let the automatic writing take over.

When you're ready to stop, set the pen down, shake out both of your hands, and then read what you've written.

You may want to save the pages and return to them a few weeks or months down the road, to see how the messages fit with your life as it's unfolding.

CONCLUSION

Ideally, no matter what form your individual spiritual practice takes, the act of honoring and celebrating the Wheel of the Year should be viewed as an art, rather than a rigid, unchanging routine.

A dynamic, creative and evolving approach to connecting with Nature and the divine is at the heart of Wicca and other modern branches of Paganism. This guide was written in that spirit, offering insight and information that will hopefully help you to build your own unique relationship with the Wheel of the Year.

As you progress along your path from one season to the next, the Sabbats provide regular opportunities to learn and grow in your faith. And as the years go by, the experience of "turning the Wheel" becomes richer and more rewarding. Indeed, the wise among us say that you are never done learning, so by all means don't stop your Sabbat education at the end of this guide.

As a next step in expanding your knowledge, you might check out some of the resources listed on the following page. And no matter where you go from here, may the God and Goddess be ever present with you on your path.

Blessed Be.

SUGGESTIONS FOR
FURTHER READING

The Wheel of the Year is truly an enormous topic, with so many variations among traditions and individuals who celebrate the Sabbats.

While you'll no doubt find some similar information in many other resources, each author has their own individual experiences and perspective on these days of power. As with anything else in Wicca or the larger Pagan world, it's always worth the effort to learn as much as you can in order to deepen your own practice.

This brief list of books offers some solid places to start. Happy reading!

Pauline Campanelli, *Wheel of the Year: Living the Magical Life* (1989)

Eileen Holland, *The Spellcaster's Reference: Magickal Timing for the Wheel of the Year* (2009)

Edain McCoy, *Sabbats: A Witch's Approach to Living the Old Ways* (2002)

Judy Ann Nock, *The Provenance Press Guide to the Wiccan Year: A Year Round Guide to Spells, Rituals, and Holiday Celebrations* (2007)

Nigel Pennick, *The Pagan Book of Days: A Guide to the Festivals, Traditions, and Sacred Days of the Year* (2009)

THREE FREE
AUDIOBOOKS PROMOTION

Don't forget, you can now enjoy **three audiobooks completely free of charge** when you start a free 30-day trial with Audible.

If you're new to the Craft, *Wicca Starter Kit* contains three of Lisa's most popular books for beginning Wiccans. You can download it for free at:

www.wiccaliving.com/free-wiccan-audiobooks

Or, if you're wanting to expand your magical skills, check out *Spellbook Starter Kit,* with three collections of spellwork featuring the powerful energies of candles, colors, crystals, mineral stones, and magical herbs. Download over 150 spells for free at:

www.wiccaliving.com/free-spell-audiobooks

Members receive free audiobooks every month, as well as exclusive discounts. And, if you don't want to continue with Audible, just remember to cancel your membership. You won't be charged a cent, and you'll get to keep your books!

Happy listening!

MORE BOOKS BY
LISA CHAMBERLAIN

Wicca for Beginners: A Guide to Wiccan Beliefs, Rituals, Magic, and Witchcraft

Wicca Book of Spells: A Book of Shadows for Wiccans, Witches, and Other Practitioners of Magic

Wicca Herbal Magic: A Beginner's Guide to Practicing Wiccan Herbal Magic, with Simple Herb Spells

Wicca Book of Herbal Spells: A Book of Shadows for Wiccans, Witches, and Other Practitioners of Herbal Magic

Wicca Candle Magic: A Beginner's Guide to Practicing Wiccan Candle Magic, with Simple Candle Spells

Wicca Book of Candle Spells: A Book of Shadows for Wiccans, Witches, and Other Practitioners of Candle Magic

Wicca Crystal Magic: A Beginner's Guide to Practicing Wiccan Crystal Magic, with Simple Crystal Spells

Wicca Book of Crystal Spells: A Book of Shadows for Wiccans, Witches, and Other Practitioners of Crystal Magic

Tarot for Beginners: A Guide to Psychic Tarot Reading, Real Tarot Card Meanings, and Simple Tarot Spreads

Runes for Beginners: A Guide to Reading Runes in Divination, Rune Magic, and the Meaning of the Elder Futhark Runes

Wicca Moon Magic: A Wiccan's Guide and Grimoire for Working Magic with Lunar Energies

Wicca Wheel of the Year Magic: A Beginner's Guide to the Sabbats, with History, Symbolism, Celebration Ideas, and Dedicated Sabbat Spells

Wicca Kitchen Witchery: A Beginner's Guide to Magical Cooking, with Simple Spells and Recipes

Wicca Essential Oils Magic: A Beginner's Guide to Working with Magical Oils, with Simple Recipes and Spells

Wicca Elemental Magic: A Guide to the Elements, Witchcraft, and Magical Spells

Wicca Magical Deities: A Guide to the Wiccan God and Goddess, and Choosing a Deity to Work Magic With

Wicca Living a Magical Life: A Guide to Initiation and Navigating Your Journey in the Craft

Magic and the Law of Attraction: A Witch's Guide to the Magic of Intention, Raising Your Frequency, and Building Your Reality

Wicca Altar and Tools: A Beginner's Guide to Wiccan Altars, Tools for Spellwork, and Casting the Circle

Wicca Finding Your Path: A Beginner's Guide to Wiccan Traditions, Solitary Practitioners, Eclectic Witches, Covens, and Circles

Wicca Book of Shadows: A Beginner's Guide to Keeping Your Own Book of Shadows and the History of Grimoires

Modern Witchcraft and Magic for Beginners: A Guide to Traditional and Contemporary Paths, with Magical Techniques for the Beginner Witch

FREE GIFT REMINDER

Just a reminder that Lisa is giving away an exclusive, free spell book as a thank-you gift to new readers!

Little Book of Spells contains ten spells that are ideal for newcomers to the practice of magic, but are also suitable for any level of experience.

Read it on read on your laptop, phone, tablet, Kindle or Nook device by visiting:

<u>www.wiccaliving.com/bonus</u>

DID YOU ENJOY
WICCA NATURAL MAGIC KIT?

Thanks so much for reading this book! I know there are many great books out there about Wicca, so I really appreciate you choosing this one.

If you enjoyed the book, I have a small favor to ask—would you take a couple of minutes to leave a review for this book on Amazon?

Your feedback will help me to make improvements to this book, and to create even better ones in the future. It will also help me develop new ideas for books on other topics that might be of interest to you. Thanks in advance for your help!

Printed in Great Britain
by Amazon